The Invisible
SOLDIER

The Invisible
SOLDIER

Captain W.A.P. Durie, His Life and Afterlife

VERONICA CUSACK

M&S

National Library of Canada Cataloguing in Publication

Cusack, Veronica
The invisible soldier : Captain W.A.P. Durie, his life and afterlife / Veronica Cusack.

ISBN 1-55199-094-6

1. Durie, W. A. P. (William Arthur Peel), 1881-1917. 2. Durie, Anna, 1856-1933.
3. World War, 1914-1918. 4. Durie, W. A. P. (William Arthur Peel),
1881-1917 — Death and burial. 5. Soldiers — Canada — Biography.
6. Toronto (Ont.) — Biography. I. Title.

FC27.D87C88 2004   971.3'54103'0922   C2004-900968-0

We acknowledge the financial support of the Government of Canada through the
Book Publishing Industry Development Program and that of the Government
of Ontario through the Ontario Media Development Corporation's Ontario
Book Initiative. We further acknowledge the support of the Canada Council for
the Arts and the Ontario Arts Council for our publishing program.

Typeset in Bembo by M&S, Toronto
Printed and bound in Canada

This book is printed on 50% post-consumer waste recycled paper

McClelland & Stewart Ltd.
The Canadian Publishers
481 University Avenue
Toronto, Ontario
M5G 2E9
www.mcclelland.com

1 2 3 4 5   08 07 06 05 04

To my own sons
James and David

CONTENTS

PREFACE

So much and so little information all at once.

It was in a coffee shop that I first heard mention of the grave robbing. R.H. Thomson had recently completed the narration of *For King & Empire*, a television series about World War I, and told me the strange tale of Anna Durie and her son. Norm Christie's book, the inspiration for the series, gave only a brief synopsis of the matter and generated yet more questions. Who was this woman, and who was the man she quite literally adored?

Army personnel papers show only the briefest glimpse of Captain William Arthur Peel Durie of the 58th Battalion, Canadian Expeditionary Force. And the battalion's War Diary, a record of each day's battles, baths, soccer matches, and deaths, mentions him only twice – one of those being grossly inaccurate.

My research moved on to hours of telephone conversations with the Commonwealth War Graves Commission in England. Kevin Shackleton, author of *Second to None: The Fighting 58th Battalion of the Canadian Expeditionary Force*, was generosity itself in allowing access to his detailed files, including a store of letters and diaries from Durie's fellow officers. But it was still not enough.

And then my discovery. Five boxes of family papers catalogued and stashed away in the City of Toronto Archives. On the morning they were trundled into the reading room I had no idea what was inside – perhaps fifty years of dinner menus. I opened the first: letters. World War I letters signed by Durie, his mother, Anna, and his sister, Helen. There was supposed to be quiet in the hushed, climate-controlled room. The clerk at the desk gave a tight smile at my exclamation and asked, "Is that a good 'Holy shit' or a bad 'Holy shit'?" A good one, definitely a good one.

The boxes held a slew of documents: mortgages, photographs, spirit writing, notebooks, wills, and two novels written by Anna, one of which is an idealized portrait of her own family. The scores of letters were seeded among the pages of her unfinished memoir, *A Canadian Volunteer*. I wrote an eight-thousand-word article for *Toronto Life* magazine. A book publisher came to call, and so there followed trips to the CWGC's British office to view the thick Durie file and learn yet more of this story. I crossed the Channel to weep my way through the graveyards and battlegrounds of the Western Front.

But no matter how great the research, a further recitation of fact would not suffice. Anna Durie's poems and memoir detail her soldier son as a mythic hero, yet he is absent from any list of honours and medals. She describes a man whose existence I could not discover. An invisible man.

Captain Durie made a choice. He insisted this book be written in his own voice. Anna, too, needed to explain. This is the story they told me.

PART ONE

ARTHUR'S WAR

3 p.m. November 20th, /15
Dining Car, "Frontenac"
58th Battalion C.E.F.
International Railway
Just passed Prescott

My dearest Mother,
You don't know how grieved I was to have missed you this morning. I looked everywhere for you but could not find you in the dark. We left in two parts, (C Company was in the second half,) at 4.45 a.m. from just behind the poultry building. I sent you two messages, one by my batman's sister, and one, just as we pulled into the Union Station, by a stranger. I am not feeling in the best of spirits, but I suppose I will cheer up as I get on our journey. There are sixteen cars in this train and the meals are excellent for officers and men. I will write to you as often as I can for the fountain pen that Helen gave me is a beauty. Everything is running smoothly and we mail letters at every town we pass. Give my love to dearest Helen.

Your affectionate son,

W.A.P. Durie

ARTHUR

I am supposed to be my father's son. Since I was a tiny child it was clear to my mother I was to be the warrior, like the warriors in the tales she told me all through my childhood. I am a Durie. Descended from military greatness. But I don't feel great. Or noble. Or particularly brave. I'm not a leader of men. I was promoted to captain only because there are spaces to fill as people keep dying. When I talk, other officers tend to drift into more interesting conversations happening just to the left. When I give battle orders the men's eyes wander the landscape. No one is rude. A lot of them quite like me. But I once heard Arnie Jukes refer to me as "ineffectual." Jukes was trolling for volunteers on one of his let's-lob-some-grenades missions, so I wasn't too bothered by the remark. Anyway, it's true. Ineffectual is a fitting description. I do my work; I try to be a good man; I care deeply for those under my command. But I am powerless to keep them from harm.

When I set off for the front I thought it would be a big adventure. Of course I knew of the slaughter. Soldiers tramping forward in neat formation, conveniently lined up for the German machine guns. The Hun didn't even have to aim, just rake along the line, and the men fell in their hundreds. But still that carnage didn't seem as if it would be part of *my* war. I imagined brave warriors dying with a splash of red on the tunic and a wry smile on the lips and, if the pain was really bad, a muffled oath.

It's difficult to look back on the Lieutenant William Arthur Peel Durie who marched into Belgium. He thought he knew everything. Now I understand nothing. I'd been in a militia unit in Toronto. Weekends and holidays spent at training camp in Niagara. And I'd worked in the Royal Bank for fifteen years, adding up figures, making sure the decimal point was in the right place, imposing the security of order. Training with the 58th Battalion wasn't all that different. I liked to be meticulous, disciplined; others saw me as demanding, even dainty. More than one officer called me "Mrs. Durie," usually in my hearing. But they didn't understand; it wasn't a matter of wanting the rules followed, the buttons polished. It was about hiding. I enveloped myself in regulations and empty formalism in order to disguise the uncertainties. Pretending I was a leader so I wouldn't have to admit I was anything else.

In my mother's bedtime stories there existed a young man who arrived at King Arthur's court ignorant of his own identity. He'd grown up in the northlands, gently bred and an excellent horseman, anxious to find his rightful place in the world. But his mother ruled those lands without a husband and refused to tell her son his own name. To be nameless is a frightening state, for our true name holds our true being. And so the knights dubbed him Le Bel Inconnu, the Fair Unknown. In order to discover his spirit and to name it, the youth had first to undertake fearful trials. He entered the Forest Perilous where dwelt ghastly beings and wailing bodiless voices.

This is my first trip abroad. Thirty-four years old before I had the nerve to leave Canada. My mother and sister travelled to Europe in the summer of 1914. I declined the invitation to accompany them, explaining that "the political situation has made everything unsettled in the financial world." Pressures of work meant I had to stay in Toronto. I was a clerk! My financial world consisted of making sure the cashbook balanced at the end of each day. But the reasoning sufficed. I didn't have to face the turmoil and responsibility of travel, and my mother could enjoy the delusion of my importance. Such excuses cannot be considered lies. They simply oiled the wheels of our life together. I love her very much but there is a game we play, and recently its rules have changed. She used to protect me. Now I protect her, whatever she thinks to the contrary. I tell her anecdotes, a little gossip; I say nothing of my real life. Her place has been usurped. Now I am protected by the thunder that surrounds me. It is bigger than me and rescues me, growling, proud, godlike, putting me in my place, taking away my responsibility, wrapping me up in its giant hand. The thunder calms me, frees me from the terror of mattering.

Bramshott Camp,
Sunday, December 12th,
1915.
8:30 p.m.

My dearest Mother,
I am writing today in the hope that this letter will reach you by
Christmas Day and I wish you and dearest Helen a very Merry

Christmas and Happy New Year. I shall be going up to London very soon. We have got pretty well settled down here, and the first half of the men have gone on six days' leave. I have not yet been sent on a course; but I shall probably get one in about a month's time. To-day the weather has been very much colder and I like it much better. I think I mentioned the 41st Battalion, (French Canadian) in one of my letters. They have been behaving very badly; getting us in wrong with the people about here. Things culminated the other day when one of the sergeants in the 9th Canadian Mounted Rifles was murdered and an officer in the 41st by the name of Coderre was arrested; some relation to one of the Canadian Cabinet Ministers. They took them all away from here to Aldershot and everyone here is happy that they have gone. The 37th Battalion has taken their place.

We have had a good deal of sickness among the men on account of the dampness. Whenever I go out for a walk I notice the absence of men about here; they have cleared the country pretty well of men. I forgot to tell you that the Army Service Corps use mules everywhere; it seems so funny to see them. Send me as much news as you can. A few of our officers have been under the weather with colds. We do not get nearly as much war news as you get in Canada. Prices are very very high; they soak Canadians whenever they see them but apart from that every thing is expensive; meals are much more expensive than they are in Canada, dinner is about $1.15, which is going some.

Well, dearest Mother, again I wish you and Helen a Merry Christmas.

With all the love I have,
Your affectionate son,

Arthur

· 7 ·

ARTHUR

Most of our officers spent their first leave at the Regent Palace Hotel in London, a respite from the intense training we endured in southern England. But after only a few hours I knew I couldn't remain. Their adventure was to be broader than mine. Pretty girls and easy camaraderie. Laughter, singing, trips to racy shows. Instead I went to the Junior Army and Navy Club in Whitehall: very staid, very quiet. Convincing myself this was just the sort of place I liked. Reality was I ached to be at the Regent. I wanted to be part of that affinity, to move freely in that world of men. But I was frightened. I thought I might lose control and let slip my loneliness.

Elmo Cusler came to find me. I distrusted his overtures then. His deep grey eyes and black hair reminded me of a Spanish conquistador, and I had no idea why he would seek me out. His men adored him. He could give stirring speeches that fired the blood, then tell bawdy jokes until his listeners choked on their laughter. Woman would turn in the street to gaze after his tall, striding figure. He already was involved with a doe-eyed New Zealand girl who lived near Bramshott Camp in Hampshire. And on arrival in Flanders he personally chose an orderly-room corporal to act as his batman, a slender boy who ministered to his every need. In battle he was a wild man, yet he knew the lineage of each plant and tree and would nurture the ferns growing on the parados before carefully pressing them into letters he wrote home to his family, his "dear ones."

In the early days, when others derided my meticulous manner, Lieutenant Cusler would simply ignore whatever pompous lecture I was delivering. "Well, never mind about that now," he'd say, and propel me out of rejoinder range, supposedly to sign yet another inventory or to scan the daily divisional reports and their morale-boosting particulars. It took me a while to appreciate their alias of *Comic Cuts*, after the children's newspaper which advertised as "amusing without being vulgar."

George McNair was my more usual companion. As a captain he was one rank senior to me, eight years older, married, staid, quiet. He called me Arthur. Cusler insisted on calling me Bill. My Christian names are William Arthur Peel. The last is my mother's maiden name, and I was given my father's first name only as an honour; it was never intended to be mine. I continually corrected battalion members who called me Bill and they accepted such a correction for a while. But Cusler would have none of it.

"I know you're a Bill, Bill. You should never be called Arthur. Our task is to let Bill out. I like him." I loved him in that moment of recognition.

We left the Junior and walked to an ancient tea room on St. James. Cusler said that even its musty interior was preferable to the antediluvian specimens ensconced in my chosen club. I thought there would be raucous tales of the Regent. Instead he was content to sit and talk about his home. He told me of his family, of his love for all of nature. Of how much he enjoyed the walks around Bramshott Camp, across the wild moorland, traversing the dip of the Devil's Punch Bowl as the mist rolled across its rim.

And he told me how he wanted his tunic front to sag under the weight of medals. He wanted glory at any cost.

"After death is the only time for safety. I want to get out there, Bill. I want to fight. I want to be part of it. Anyway, what is life to me?"

In the face of his sterling passions I felt inadequate. What god would give such gifts to one man and leave another so unsure?

London, March 18th, 1916

My dearest Helen,
Arthur and I spent a very busy day yesterday, and he left, as I told you he would, on the 7:05 train in the evening, (St. Patrick's day) for Shorncliffe. It was so fortunate that two of your letters came before he left.

He bought a haversack and an officer's messing-tin, I think he called it, but he would not buy many extra things for he will have to <u>carry</u> nearly everything except his blankets and sleeping bag. I have some things here for him which I will send after him. Once or twice a week I will send him what he needs; but things must be restricted to actual personal needs. He would not take even a box of chocolates.

We went to two or three places together: the Victoria and Albert Museum; the Law Courts; the Inner Temple; the Thames Embankment and then went on to Selfridges for tea, a substantial tea, as he was leaving before dinner. We got back before six o'clock and I went with him to Charing Cross Station. He kissed me good-bye, and as the train began to move he came again to the open window and leaned out and I kissed him again. I came back home without any difficulty, and got to bed early, as I was tired. My being here has been very fortunate.

I think it would be foolish for you to send him anything; it would take so long to come. He has fifteen pairs of socks, which he will take with him, but most of his underwear will be left behind in the trunk which he will leave with me. He would not take his dunnage bag, because, he said, it would only be lost. The actual procedure is: first the buttons are removed from their uniform and privates' buttons substituted; they are given a new web equipment (quite different from the Canadian web) which includes a huge pack like a knapsack that holds the kit and is worn on the back. Arthur provided himself with a small box of ammunition for his revolver which the Government should supply, but sometimes fails to supply. It was frightfully heavy. All this has to be carried. You see how different it is from a march through the streets of Toronto. His great coat alone is weight enough, and in addition he will have his British warm. All the small accessories of his toilet go into his haversack, which, of course, is slung at the side. He will let me hear from him just as often as he can write, and he will tell me all he can.

Your loving Mother

Anna Durie

ARTHUR

From the very moment I was called to active service it was my mother's intention to follow me to France. She decided to stay in England during training, then journey as near to the front lines as possible. Something must inevitably happen to me.

Something always did happen to me. Or so she said. It was her duty to be there, to be ready.

In London she stayed in Russell Square for easy access to the Royal Bank and the French consul and began work on her mission to move into the war zone. Various officials advised she attach herself to some organization operating across the Channel. At the Canadian Red Cross the commissioner gave a diplomatic no.

"The whole trouble," he told her, "lies with the French government. There are a limited number of passes and when they are all in use, except in a very particular case, they will grant no more.

"Spies got into the canteen of the YMCA," he said. "The French government bundled them all back home and positively refused to allow more women to enter the war zone."

On his recommendation, she went to the Anglo British Hospital Association but they had much the same tale to tell. Next she visited the French Croix-Rouge. Again, no. The French consulate required that she show papers proving she was "British all through"–which, of course, she couldn't do. A pattern emerged. I suspect they were frightened she would demand a directorship. Mother does have a way of insisting she knows exactly what is best for everyone.

Finally she had to admit defeat and accept the role of distant helpmate. Does any other Canadian soldier have a mother who travelled the Atlantic to watch over him? Wives by the thousand made the trip, usually living with their once abandoned relatives. But mothers are scarce.

There was much to supervise. She ordered an ivory ID tag, it hangs on a chain around my neck; moved all the buttons on my greatcoat, as my chest had expanded under the rigours of training; sent slippers to the officers at camp; and, when I left for the front, arranged for a shipment of fingerless mittens. She made up hampers of cakes and candies for me to share, and scoured the city searching for requested medicines and books.

But all the time, as the Zeppelins moved silently over London, she waited for the "inevitable."

Somewhere in Belgium.
April 28th, 1916,
Friday, 3:30 p.m.

My dearest Mother,
I have just received your letter of April 25th, Tuesday. The pineapple arrived O.K., also the small cakes, the larger cake and the chocolates and all in good condition. Thank you so much, dearest mother. I am living with Captain Gunton our Quartermaster, and we are extremely comfortable. I got all your papers: the Pall Mall Gazette, the Times and the Evening News. It is a lovely day although it is getting a bit windy. I am sitting in the little pay office close to the wall, writing this letter. So far, to-day, there has been little firing. Captain Gunton is very kind. I am feeling much better to-day. To-morrow the Battalion goes up to the front line. We received a letter from Captain Forwood in which he said he would be back some time next week. When he comes back I will return to the Battalion. In your last letter you did not say how your cold was. Do let me know. I see by the newspapers you sent me that

there is trouble in Ireland. I suppose they will have got it under
control by this time. At least one would think so. They seem to be
letting up a little.

I am having a fairly quiet time and hope to be all right very
soon.

Your affectionate son,

W.A.P. Durie

ARTHUR

"A long, long time ago — if I were there then, I wouldn't be
there now; if I were there now and at that time, I would have
a new story or an old story, or I might have no story at all. . . ."

My mother's tales always began that way. Just as her father
had told them to her. And I would lie in my bed in that big
house where the servants dwindled and the rooms echoed,
and I would listen to her tell of heroes and heroines and how
I was the son of a hero, destined to be an even greater hero.
Now, when I think of those ancient tales, I imagine how history begins in truth and is slowly plied by age and circumstance, until it bends and folds and becomes fantastical myth.
Yet in my own life, time runs backward. I was born a mythic
hero and I grew to be a lesser man.

Six weeks after I arrived in Flanders, George McNair was
killed. My best friend. There'd been other deaths in the battalion: fourteen to that point. But this was the first time it had
suffered a direct attack. The Hun bombarded our trenches
with everything: whizz-bangs, Jack Johnsons, singing Minnies,
then with a great mass of Prussian guards swarming over their

parapets. Nine members of the 58th died and twelve others simply couldn't be found, at least not enough to positively identify. They managed to collect George's body and bury him in Maple Copse, a haphazard little cemetery next to one of the dressing stations. I visited his grave a few days later. Someone had made a Celtic cross, the kind that has a ring intersecting the shaft and crossbar. The circle is supposed to symbolize God's eternal love shown through the sacrifice of his Son. I don't believe in God any more. I prefer the more plausible explanation: they were once phallic standing stones, carved by the Druids, then reworked by zealous Christians attempting to disguise such carnality. It's appropriate for George, he had young children. Name, battalion, date of death were carefully painted onto the wood. I wrote to his wife to tell her he was well looked after, that I'd put bluebells under the cross, that she could visit him when the war was over. A month later his grave and everything in it, in fact all of the graves at Maple Copse, were obliterated by shellfire. He is scattered through the tiny graveyard. Still there, but invisible.

I didn't see George die. I wasn't in the line. They'd sent me to Divisional Reserve to act as paymaster when the regular pay officer was called to London. I didn't want to stay. Too like my days at the bank. Columns and figures and everything in perfect order. I was only an hour's walk from the battalion, well in range of the shells, but I was immersed in luxury compared with the trenches. I had a real bed and even a modicum of privacy. And the best thing was I could ride again. My father taught me to ride when I could barely walk. I remember him catching me up into his saddle without slowing the horse. I can yet capture that feeling of exhilaration. Standing very still, as he commanded, while the huge mass of dark muscle rushed toward me; then the sudden swoop through the air to land hard against my father's chest, his one arm pulling me into him. Safe. Held. And he would spur the horse as I screamed with delight, the wind snatching my voice away. The three of us one strength, one speed.

Somewhere in Belgium
April 30, 1916
Sunday, 8 a.m.

My dearest Mother,
Thank you very much for telling me about Mrs. Vankoughnet. We would appreciate the socks very much. I shall write to her at once to thank her for her kindness. The comforts will be very welcome, and you would think so too if you could see the men sleeping on the firing step at night, as I have.

Things are just running about the same. In the afternoon I rode up to the chief Paymaster's; in the evening George Curtis, who is now in charge of the Transport, asked me if I would like to go up with the ration party, and, of course, I went. I have been riding a little western pony that belonged to Major Leckie. It was a very nice, starlight night and Fritzy was very good indeed. George Curtis and I were riding at the head of the line and when he came to the dangerous part of the road he put the spurs to his horse and so did I. I thought I was going for an aeroplane ride. We got back about 1 a.m. this morning without anything happening. I had not been long in bed when the gas gong rang and an officer of the Battalion next to us put his head into our shack and shouted "Gas! Stand to!" I jumped up, cursing my luck, for I was so tired after my ride that I had not put my pyjamas on. Anyway I grabbed my gas helmet, which I always keep near, and dressed as quickly as possible. There was no gas. We stayed up for about an hour and then went to bed; but there was an awful bombardment going on. We ate your nice cake at about 2 a.m. and were very thankful indeed to have it.

It is a lovely day. This is certainly Spring, and it is certainly delightful. I am very different from what I was in the bank; my nerves are much steadier.

I am going again (riding) to the Divisional Cashier.

Good-bye, dearest Mum.

Your affectionate son,

W.A.P. Durie Lt.

ARTHUR

At Divisional Reserve I rode a yellow pony, quiet and surefooted, that could run like a deer. He'd belonged to Major Leckie, who was blown to pieces by a German crump, but he never seemed bothered by a strange rider. There were horses everywhere around the château, many looking as if they'd done more than their share in the war, and they weren't at peace even yet. Often shells would land in the fields and scatter them or maim an unlucky few.

On one part of the road into the Lille Gate at Ypres it's necessary to go at a gallop to avoid the sweep of machine gun fire. Eons ago Fritz pressed forward and tried to capture the town of Ypres. The Allies pressed back and kept on pressing across the original front line until a bulge, a salient, was formed around the town. It was a pyrrhic victory. German guns and artillery now blasted the British forces from three sides and, it seemed to those on the frequent transports, concentrated their efforts toward one point on the Zillebeke Road – Shrapnel Corner.

I loved that section of the journey to and from the town, galloping past the enemy emplacements sitting on the higher ground to the west. At times I'd race another horse and rider. Allowing the pony to go for all he was worth. Surrendering myself up to his speed, his power: knowing only the wind and the dank smell of his coat as my face pressed against his neck. My yellow pony inevitably won. Small glimmers of pleasure.

If time allowed, I'd ride through the countryside behind the town up to Mont des Cats, past hills blue with hyacinth. I'd look across to the North Sea, over tiny villages where church steeples pressed against the sky, trying desperately to ignore the scene at my back: shell holes and mud and a medieval town reduced to rubble.

Frequently I'd take messages to the senior officers hunkered down in Ypres's ancient earth-covered ramparts, seventy feet thick and fronted with a huge brick wall now scarred by shell bursts. I've seen pictures of how the town looked before the war, dominated by its fine cathedral and magnificent Cloth Hall. So full of wonder. Just a small portion of the bell tower and a scrap of west wall remain today. Graceful arches are now piles of stone. What once held Belgium's glory has taken on eccentric form, and wild poppies grow among the debris.

Before returning along the broken road, I'd sit at the edge of the marketplace, something that once was a gargoyle grinning up at me. The pony waiting patiently as I watched the throng. The square held rubble and soldiers, yet those men were walking in the footsteps of serfs and artisans and nobles. Countless generations traded in that huge plaza. Citizens who thought themselves safe behind their ramparts.

———————

Colonel Genet chose me for the paymaster position for reasons other than my ability with figures. My time in the lines had been difficult. Life was not as I expected. The army is discipline; it has to be, or chaos will ensue. Precise drill, strict march regulations, exactness in performance. Discipline should ready a soldier for any circumstance, for the silent execution of any job, perhaps in darkness and in danger only yards from the enemy. When training in Niagara and again in England, I made sure the rules were applied to the letter. If I could control my men through rigid command, then I could control myself as well.

But when we arrived in Flanders I found another world. Things I never expected. The terrible sickening smell – shit and sweat and decomposing flesh; the wall of it encountered long before we even saw the front lines. The lice that infested my body within a few days. The rats that ran across me as I tried to sleep. And the weather. The first month, March of 1916, saw the heaviest rainfall in Flanders in thirty-five years. Our greatest struggle was not with the enemy, it was with the mud.

The stink, the vermin, the water up to our thighs, no adequate clothing, impossible to keep dry or warm. And a constant stream of messages from HQ wanting us to count the notepads or report on the tinned jam situation. Didn't they understand our conditions? What was their reasoning? Now I know those Staff officers hold on to the mentality I carried with me in training. Everything to the letter. Order and inventory. They rarely move from behind a desk. They are distinguished from our khaki, which blends into the mud, by the wearing of red shoulder tabs and hat bands. The Red Badge of Funk.

I had no answers. Confused by everything and everyone, I threw myself into work. A subaltern's duties in the trenches are principally conducted at night: supervising repair work or the bringing up of supplies; walking the line to see the sentries aren't asleep; leading patrols out into no man's land to reconnoitre the enemy or lay down yet more barbed wire, acres of it. You have to jump over the parapet. It seemed so strange to be out in front and to see our men and the Germans firing at one another, as if I'd shrunk to the size of a flea and was crouched on a child's game board watching the incomprehensible doings of humans. Saps are out there: old shell holes mostly, used as listening posts to try to discover what Fritz is up to. Every two hours they are relieved and it's customary for the officer on duty to visit. Saying it so easily makes it sound like a leisurely stroll to the corner store. It's not, believe me. But as nervous as I felt, it was as nothing compared with the terrors of the man in that hole. Completely alone. Every creak of the wire, every rat scurrying between the lines sounding like an enemy patrol. I would arrive at the edge of his mud pit, whispering some code word to let him know I was friendly, and I would see an ashen face and a man who hadn't drawn breath in the agony of hearing my footfalls.

One night, my final night of such duties for some time, I was on my way back to our lines, desperately trying to be quiet as my boots made sucking noises in the mud. I heard the echo coming back to me across the mire. There are worlds beyond our own, inhabited by godlings and fairy folk and fetches, places where monsters stalk the heroes and where fantastical creatures possess powers we can barely imagine. Sometimes the inhabitants of those worlds cross into the land of men – to harm us, to play with us, to help us. I'm not insane. I have seen things.

In the pitch of darkness dwells a nightwalker, a huge dog, black as coal, with eyes of fire. His name is Shriker. To hear the hideous squelching sounds of his giant paws is to hear death approaching. He prowls through the countryside searching for lone travellers who should be home safe in their beds. I would swear I heard him that night. Other sounds accompanied my own. I listened, tried to gauge their direction, willed my limbs to run. But as I barrelled forward, something wound around my ankle, and I tumbled. A knot of fabric refusing to budge, hooked into the ground. I tugged hard. In the faint moonlight an arm rose up in silhouette against the sky. I sawed frantically at the cloth with my trench knife as slime, erstwhile flesh, fell from the bone, from a limb that once held child or lover.

I lurched upright, attempting to suppress the rising vomit. Suddenly a man was in front of me. A living man. No, a boy. A short country boy, the blush of the fields still on his face. His rifle aimed at my chest, his body taut. He wore the uniform of a German private. I could feel the tremors running across my skin. My jaw was clenched shut in an attempt to prevent it being shaken from my skull. The boy too was terrified. He was staring at an officer, almost a generation older than him, perhaps a seasoned soldier. Then, as he watched, his fear turned to puzzlement. His gun lowered a little, his stance relaxed, and his face dissolved into a derisive grin.

"*Hosenscheisser.*" A snorted laugh and a grunt of wonder.

"*Hosenscheisser*," he repeated.

I knew enough German to translate. Pants shitter. Coward. I couldn't fault his deduction. I was paralyzed with fear. Staring at my own death. Not in some noble battle but in this lonely meeting with a boy. He pushed at my chest with the rifle until I stumbled a little. He smiled. We were going to play a game. He lifted the barrel, rubbing it slowly along the line of my jaw. fitting it perfectly into my right ear, then dragging around the nape of my neck as his body circled mine. He raised himself onto his toes and placed his lips against my lobe.

"*Hosenscheisser*," he repeated, drunk on the power of his gun and the darkness.

"English officer." The words were spoken softly, enunciated carefully, the syllables drawn into a caress. A wet tongue lapped into the whorls of my ear.

His hand slid down my stomach, cupped my cock, and squeezed.

My fist flew up in something between a punch and a shove, a useless gesture of defiance that ended up smacking against the curve of his neck. He stared at me with an expression of disbelief. As if I were rudely rebuffing simple overtures of friendship. Then my hand was hot, as his artery emptied into the well of my palm and his blood flowed over my wrist and along my forearm. His weight on the knife grew and I could feel the blade slide through his neck until he was cantilevered to one side, my knife wedged against his jawbone. And still he stared at me. Accusing me of such betrayal. I dragged my hand away, my breath rasping, and he crumpled, twitching at my feet. I left him there. Alone. Waiting for Shriker. And walked with no idea of direction until I rolled across a sandbag parapet to land at the feet of a middle-aged corporal, closer to shooting me than ever the German boy was. I found an empty funk hole and sat, shaking. All I needed was a little time to regain control. My hand and half my sleeve glistened red. There'd been no bravery, no skill involved. I didn't even realize what I was doing. He was simply a boy wanting a sexual thrill to accompany his killing. I've learned that such a combination is not uncommon.

First Gerry Cosbie, the medical officer, came to me. Someone must have sent for him, a message about Durie trembling in a funk hole, covered in blood. But I didn't want him to touch me. I held the knife up to show what had happened and he backed away. Cusler arrived. He wasn't interested in the knife or in an explanation. Instead he walked me to the dugout and said it was time to get cleaned up. He peeled off my tunic and my shirt and washed my hand. Then he changed the water and washed my face. I was too ashamed to tell him the story. The boy had stared so accusingly at me. He was hardly more than a child. I began to cry. Cusler held me.

"You have to be able to look at a thing, Bill, and yet not see it."

And I remembered something. Rough fabric, safety within a man's strong arms.

ANNA

In New Orleans, where I spent my childhood, only the poor receive an in-ground burial. Instead tiered vaults rise along the cemetery pathways. Rows upon rows of them; elaborate memorials flickering with votive lights. Cities of the Dead. The water table is so high, the ground so sodden, bodies will not stay within the soil. Even if the coffins are weighted they still refuse to rest, bobbing to the surface after rainstorms, rotting and thrusting their shards into the air, opening bones and fetid flesh to living eyes. As a child I saw them. I know their fate.

My little sister, Emily, and I once sneaked among those hushed corridors when our nurse, Marie, visited her ailing mother near the Bayou St. John. Papa had forbidden the trip but I persuaded her I would not tell. The strange food offered to us in her parents' house was unpalatable and there were dozens of people crowded into the tiny rooms, their presence threatening the stability of the thin walls. The old lady did not speak. She stared at us from her black eyes and I recognized the hatred. A thick yellow paste oozed along the top of her nightgown and down into the folds of grey skin. A high, sweet smell enveloped the bed. I demanded to play outside. We were told to stay near, but what could they do? Papa would sack Marie if he knew she disobeyed his wishes and took us to such a neighbourhood.

I wanted to explore. I wanted to know what happened in the forbidden places. Marie had hinted of voodoo rituals and wild dancing. She said there is an eternal crossroads over which all souls must pass on their way to the afterlife and it is guarded by a god who possesses all the knowledge of all the dead. I would sneak up on him and see his face. I would learn of these things.

We tiptoed through the narrow avenues of the St. Louis Cemetery, fascinated by the stoneworks' shapes and variety. We walked as if we were giants in a fantastical metropolis. Sarcophagus stacked on sarcophagus, fronted with curlicues and fretwork. A silent city. There were rustlings in the wet grass, and the bright sun created freakish shadows that did not match the curious tombs. Emily was scared and wanted to go back but I pulled her forward along a rutted turnoff. I refused to be afraid.

The first graves we came upon were newly made, adorned with flowers, the scent of jasmine sweetening the air. Deeper along the track, the mounds were topped only by slabs of cracked stone. A smell of dying vegetation and wild things unknown crawled across the green grass, a rich green, darker than elsewhere.

Then we saw the rotting boxes, scraps of faded fabric. Hanks of coarse hair trailed across a slat of broken wood. I wanted to know its texture. And if hair and clothing were here, what form did the soul take as it passed over the eternal crossroads? I edged forward. The grey tresses were attached not to a discernible skull but to the pale gobbet of a face that seemed made of melted candle wax, the features running one into the other, everything smooth and yellow except for a

bristle patch of blackness on the right temple. My eyes travelled below the vanishing features to a thick pool of feculence,
liquefied flesh dotted with white pustules. I tried to turn away,
but my feet slid on the slick ground and one hand punched
against that foulness and sank inside, releasing a vile stench that
welled into my eyes, my throat. Emily screamed, her sound
blotting out everything except the high-pitched laughter coming from behind the trees. I ran, as I have never run before, and
I swear the shadows watched us as we fled. Marie lost her place
in our house; Emily and I were beaten with the rod; Mama
burned my dress and would not speak to me of its stains.

In times when there is a surfeit of dying in New Orleans,
families are allowed to remove coffins from the aboveground
vaults and replace them with those of the newly dead. The old
remains are put in burlap bags and stuffed into the corners.
The bags smear mottled and dank, as decomposition contin-
ues. I am now like one of those rank containers. Rotting from
the inside. The putrescence marking my flesh, displaying my
sin. My father taught me that heaven is eternal existence in the
presence of God. Then hell is eternity without my son. I will
not join him in the afterlife. God has refused forgiveness.

London
May 4th, 1916

My dearest Helen,
Now that the newspapers are letting news through, Ireland has been such an absorbing topic that everything else has taken second place, even the Compulsion Bill. There are lots of shirkers and slackers in England as well as Canada; but here the public is determined to get them out of munition works and other employments where they have taken refuge.

There seems to have been comparative calm on the western front. Arthur's letters are so cheerful now that you realize the strain he was under when he first went over. Captain Forwood is still in England. If his position were offered to Arthur in France I wish he would take it; but I was careful to tell him to use his own judgement. I said that promotion to Captaincy took my fancy.

I have got myself in such a rut here sending Arthur letters and parcels that I don't seem to be able to get away from it. Mrs. Rose is staying on in the hope of finding a nice place in the suburbs. When she finds an inexpensive place it turns out to be so frightfully down-at-heel that she comes back utterly disheartened and saying things about English ways. The nice places within easy distance of London are all expensive. I had a nice letter from Mrs. McKeand. She has had a house with a friend but is coming back to London this week.

Your loving mother,

Anna Durie

ARTHUR

In a green land at the edge of the world, centuries before our time on this earth, lived Prince Mael Duin and his brothers. They were reared in one cradle, on one breast and in one lap. But when he became a man, Mael Duin learned his father was Ailill Edge-of-Battle, a great warrior burned alive by the sea raiders of Leix, and his real mother stayed cloistered in a convent, haunted by sadness. Mael Duin swore vengeance. He built a three-skinned boat to journey amid the Blessed Isles and search for his father's murderers.

"What is a three-skinned boat?" I asked my mother. "Where are the Blessed Isles? Who are the sea raiders of Leix?"

She put her finger to her lips. "Shush. You will live your life and learn of all the things the stories tell."

Drifting on the current, Mael Duin landed at an island of yew and willow trees. Black-skinned people walked within the wood, softly sobbing, keening, weeping into their black clothes. The crew cast lots and sent one man to ask the cause of their sorrow. A young woman came forward and touched his hand, leading him toward the trees. He began to tremble and looked back toward his shipmates, his eyes filled with longing. As they watched, his skin darkened and the woman cast a cloak and hood about his shoulders so he was indistinguishable from the rest. Mael Duin sent men after him, warning them not to speak to any of the mourners nor even to look at them. But they were unable to find the young man. He had melded into the sorrowful crowds, overtaken by their pain. He would never again walk the green land at the edge of the world. The ship sailed away and left him sobbing, keening, weeping – forever separate from his own people.

————————

On a warm night in early May, I rode at the head of the transport past Sanctuary Wood, where the battalion held the line. The area had long ceased to be either sanctuary or wood and was merely blasted kindling raked by German fire. I was about to set my pony to gallop, about to allow his speed to conquer any fears, when a bullet whined past my ear. I twisted away, but another thudded into my shoulder and I dropped to the road. I swear that as I fell Mercutio's words ran through my brain, "A plague on both your houses." I apologize if that seems pretentious. My store of profanities had not yet surfaced.

One of the sergeants rushed forward, dragging me away from the horses' hooves and the wagon wheels. The wound hurt like buggery, but it was as nothing compared with the rolling red waves of insanity inside my chest, dragging through me at every breath. The morphia tablets I carried in my gas helmet had rolled away into darkness. We were far from any medical help and the sergeant said I must drink brandy for the pain. I resisted, not because I objected to the liquor but because opening my mouth caused me to breathe and breathing caused yet more insanity. The sergeant, determined to be off the roadway as quickly as possible, had his own ideas. This was no time to mollycoddle prissy officers. He forced the flask between my lips, hissing, "This isn't a fucking Sunday school picnic." I gasped as it raked down my throat, screamed, took another breath, screamed again. And on it went.

The medical officer, Cosbie, was busy in the front line, so they loaded me onto the ration railway and trundled me off to meet him. I moved in and out of consciousness, fully waking only when Cosbie poked into my shoulder with a branding iron.

"Fuck you!" I roared.

He was twenty-one, the son of poor Irish immigrants. And already he was a doctor, accelerated through his final year at the University of Toronto. At Niagara Camp in Ontario he'd made it clear he disliked my assumption of privilege and I, in turn, was jealous of how easily he acquired friends, learning, respect. To compensate I flaunted my breeding, my manners. He answered with mimicry: a farcical rendition of Durie the moronic officer. He and Dick Joyce, his constant companion, would double over with laughter. Snorting with the brilliance of it all. I can't fault them. I was such a prig: complaining when Cosbie sneaked pure alcohol to some of the officers, lecturing them on responsibility and morality. Now I was in his hands.

He smiled at my swearing, as if I were the vicar's idiot child. "It's going to be just fine. I promise you. You're going to be right as rain within a few days." I read that false smile. I was every New Englishman who'd ever kept his ancestors beyond the Pale. Perhaps I should have tried to placate him, but all I knew was the pain, and I practised every swear word I'd heard in the previous weeks to get him to stop lacerating my shoulder and instead treat the agony in my chest. He told me not to make such a fuss. To him, there was an obvious flesh wound and a mummy's boy who wouldn't bear it like a man. My request for a second opinion came out only as bellows and profanities. I couldn't get breath into my body and the struggle to try was agonizing. I was face down in a sump, drowning. No one noticed. I flailed and struggled and tried to shout but nobody could see I was even there. I hated him. I hated everyone around me. Everyone who never looked, who never listened. Who decided in a moment who I was and judged me accordingly. Who never asked why. All my life people couldn't be bothered to see. I was invisible to them. I was invisible to him.

Cosbie slapped on a dressing and gave me a dose of morphia. I could feel the sneer down through his fingers. His report would read "Lieut. W.A.P. Durie wounded slightly." He drew a blue *M* (morphia given) on my forehead for the benefit of the next medical man. Even the drag of the pencil was agony and my opinion of his skills grew louder and more detailed. He sent me off to the dugout to await my turn for transport to Casualty Clearing.

Five hours; three men holding me down through my chaos. Mild "Mrs." Durie called heaven's curses on nearby soldiers, innocent officers, Colonel Genet, Sir Douglas Haig, every German, every batman, and every flag wagger. Their parentage, their sisters' morals, and their own genitalia were all questioned. I'm told I dredged up Latin, French, and German profanities, even "The bloody dog is dead," which caused great glee when I was reading *Richard III* as a snot-nosed schoolboy. It seems some of my more colourful clauses were much repeated, and for some time poor Cosbie was known among the officers as Dr. Knob Rot. I have no memory of such behaviour. To me the experience was pain, and intense pain gives no quarter to delicacy. When someone spoke to me and expected a reply, when they jostled against me, when they soothed my fucking brow, I simply told people to please not do that. Or a vague approximation.

I know at some point Cusler came in and took his turn at holding me steady. He sat on my legs and told me stories. I recall the low murmur of his voice pushing through the agony. Six weeks later, on the day I transferred to a hospital in England, he suffered a serious leg wound. I wonder if anyone murmured words of solace into his pain. One night at Étaples General Hospital I suddenly recalled his bulk straddling my thighs and with the memory came tales of ancient warriors smearing monkshood on their spears to ensure the enemy an agonizing death, and of women spreading a salve of henbane onto their skin, causing them to imagine broomstick flights through the night sky. He laughed about it later, said I was wild, and so told me of the wildness of nature, of how virginal buttercups and daffodils and lilies of the valley displayed their corruption, became the slayers of innocence. Wild flowers as murderers instead of the bullets and bombs of our world. He said I quieted for a while and he was sure I lay there pondering how to use such poisons on a bayonet. I think it was the weight of him that calmed me, the warmth of him that shaded my pain, his solidness giving me comfort.

Casualty Clearing looked more closely and realized the bullet had travelled inward from the shoulder, passing directly through the right lung and coming to rest in the pleural bag of the left. I was listed as "dangerously ill" and shifted to hospital. "May be visited" appeared on my chart – army talk for "about to die."

ANNA

I had been in London a little over two months and was dressing for dinner when the Swedish maid came into my room with a telegram, the one everyone in England with men at the front had learned to dread. Thousands of waiting women know what it means to receive them.

The telegram was from the chaplain at Clearing Station No. 10, Poperhinghe. Arthur was wounded. Without the loss of a moment I made my preparations. Neither letter nor words can give expression to the misery of days in that unforgettable and difficult time.

A new-born sense of my own impotence consumed me as the journey to Folkestone was begun. I had a racking, English cough and was physically very tired. My mind envisaged Arthur's face at the end of the journey calm, white and solemn in death.

My first question on landing at Boulogne was whether there was a telegram. There was none, and I was given the assurance that Arthur was probably alive.

I was put into a motor by officials of the YMCA and driven through a furious downpour of rain a distance of eighteen miles to Étaples, passing acres and acres of huts on our way: hospital wards filled to capacity with wounded officers and men. At last the motor stopped at a group of huts with a white sign bearing the inscription in large black letters "24th General Hospital." Arthur was sitting up in bed and I could hear his heavy breathing as I entered the ward; his face was pinched and drawn, his skin seemed tightened over his cheekbones.

His breath came with such difficulty that he could speak only in gasps. His hand closed on mine but speech was too great an effort, and a frequent expectoration of blood made me urge him to desist.

I am afraid there were times he proved an unruly patient. As the days passed and he got better, he grew more accustomed to the noise of passing engines and the railway traffic that moved incessantly in front of the hospital. Then, all of a sudden, he began as rapidly to lose ground until at one time there was little hope of his recovery. For a few days his temperature went higher and higher.

"Unfortunately his heart is playing out." When I returned to his bedside after having heard these words from the medical officer, Arthur exclaimed, "Mother, they've scared you stiff"; then he added, "I'm not going to die."

As he grew stronger there were heavenly days in the hospital ward. The orderly brought tea and we chatted and read the newspapers. I kept his table well supplied with flowers, which were plentiful, and delicious fruit could readily be obtained – strawberries set in neat little rows of two dozen berries in neat little boxes at five francs each.

In the next bed lay Captain Ashley, grandson of the late Earl of Enniskillen, who was shot through the base of the spine at Ypres. Dead now, but I remember him as such a handsome young man. His mother, Lady Alice Ashley, always had a smile for Arthur and an inquiry after his health.

While I was there, the Princess Helena Victoria of Schleswig-Holstein-Sonderburg-Augustenburg, granddaughter of Queen Victoria, and head of the YMCA stayed at the organization's accommodation, a delightful villa set in a perfect garden. She was most courteous and even called at Arthur's bedside on one occasion to wish him well.

ARTHUR

When the "inevitable" occurred, Mother realigned the planets in order to cross the Channel. By the time she arrived I was a patient at the military hospital in Étaples and, I regret, a disruptive one. I know the nurses were relieved at her arrival, hoping her presence would calm me. Treatment for my wound demanded that I sit upright for twelve days; it had not made for comfort. The pain was great and morphia a rare commodity, administered only when my moans and cries disturbed the other patients. I slept in fitful spans, waking to see the convoys of wounded streaming across the corridor. Their wounds were hideous.

A week before I was transferred to London, a Canadian officer arrived at the ward. His right arm was badly mangled and for the first day there was silence from his bed, punctuated by the occasional murmured "Praise God, from whom all blessings flow; / Praise Him, all creatures here below; / Praise Him above, ye heavenly host; / Praise Father, Son, and Holy Ghost."

He was of the Princess Patricia's, in the line near Ypres where the 58th still lingered. I knew nothing of their circumstances. News filters slowly and often erroneously, and anyway I'd been a little preoccupied. The next afternoon, his doxology grew louder and blossomed into a full-throated tenor rendition, repeated and repeated and repeated. An elderly visitor asked him to please be a little quieter. He stared at the man for a full minute, forcing him to avert his eyes, then began to recite a litany of names and the condition in which he'd last seen each of his comrades. They'd come under a vicious artillery assault, the beginning of the battle for Mount Sorrel. Soldiers blown into the air, returning earthward in pieces. His details were exact, a duplication of the images embedded in his brain. The noise continued to rise until it boomed across the ward. Mother laid her hand on his arm and asked him to lower his voice. She feared he would cause the nurses to clear all visitors for the day. He was oblivious to her request. By then he was weeping, his fingers plucking at his damp skin, as he spewed out the roster. I watched the spittle drooling along his chin, mixing with his tears, and wondered how my comrades were faring. I was eating strawberries, lying between clean sheets; they remained in the Salient trenches. The officer slid from his bed onto the linoleum. Names were no longer discernible, his weeping had turned into a blubbering of mucus and heaving sobs. I knew this person. I recognized his visions. All eyes were turned away from him, from what they saw as his shame. This was not the way an officer of the king behaves. A doctor and an orderly escorted him from the ward and my mother tut-tutted her sorrow that such a fine figure of a man should possess so unstable a mind. She wondered if he had perhaps been promoted from the lower ranks.

———

In London, in a ward overlooking Hyde Park, the doctors told us my lung would never fully heal and an operation for the extraction of the bullet could not be undertaken. The risk was too great. The only treatment was breathing exercises, a healthy manner of living, and a long convalescence. When I recovered sufficiently to leave my bed I was allowed to lie on a wicker couch on the rooftop and watch the horses and their riders on Rotten Row. Daylight saving time was introduced that year and evenings with my mother were long lingering discussions in the soft light. We would talk until the darkness overtook us. Most of our chat was of memories, or dreams of when the war was over. She complained about the slang I'd picked up while in Europe, my "lazy" way of talking. And she repeatedly spoke of the promotion and Staff position that would be mine away from the front. I told her and I told her: I was *not* going back to Canada and I was *not* taking a job in London; instead I was returning to the battalion as soon as able. I had a job to do. She assured me my health would never sufficiently recover, that there was no doubt as to the course nature would force me to pursue. I never wavered. Neither did she.

Helen, freed for the holidays from her teaching position at Jarvis Collegiate, arrived in the summer. She fretted over my gaunt figure and laboured breathing. I was shocked by how tired she obviously was, almost defeated. She has assumed so many of my burdens. Mother had protested at her pursuing an undergraduate degree, then a master's degree, and finally at her taking up a profession. She saw no reason why a girl of her breeding would choose such a path. Helen is a gentlewoman who must marry well and save her strength for bearing children! And presumably the bills will be paid by the Good Fairy!

Helen was at my bedside when Cusler hobbled into the ward. His third visit since the doctors gave in to his loud protestations of death by boredom and allowed him crutches and afternoon outings. He charmed my sister immediately. His tall frame curving into the conversation, a lopsided shy smile – how he pulls that one off I don't know – a firm handshake lingering an instant past propriety. This was Helen's first meeting with him. She was not a girl any more but I suspect her experience was as non-existent as mine. Mother has reserved Helen for some great man, and time in London would allow her to meet with the most eligible of officers; but I have seen blue-blooded ladies fall beneath Cusler's spell. Helen was lost.

1st Lon Gen Hosp
St Gabriels College
Camberwell Str
27/6/16

My dear ones,
This is a great war. I am sure some warrior. Anyway I can play the part of the invalid to the height of perfection. I get out every day in a spinal bed. I can sit up and throw my wooden leg around in great style. You see I have my foot in a splint. As for the hip, it's fine, never know I had a wound but I will carry a little German weight along with me as there is still a small piece of shell in my thigh that will never do any harm and it will save another operation. My little colonial (New Zealander) was up to see me Sunday and brought me some beautiful roses and some luscious strawberries. Some class!

Eh! What! And best of all her mother sent a special invitation down for me to convalesce at their home. I am afraid to take a chance, she is too sweet a little baby to be around me. I am afraid I would be tempted to marry the girl and then I would hate to have to go back to the front. We have a great ward. We have all been given flowers and besides we took a collection and gave the money to the day sister to purchase flowers for us so we are all decked out like a xmas tree. They say we have the best ward in the house and they have 1100 beds here so that is going some. Of course we are those damned Canadians so why wonder. The day sister and the night nurse are sure fine, no particular Hellers to look at, but the best by far at that and they are human but I can't go too strong on the rest of the animals we have. By the way my kit is here from France so that is pretty good time. I will have to check it up and see what I have.

I see we got messed up a little the day after I left. We had 4 of our officers killed and 2 wounded. I got a letter from our quarter master and he said "well Mr Cusler you are lucky to get off as easy as you did" and believe me I quite agree with him. Life is sweet and I saw a few lopped off let me tell you, but she is a game of chance. You flip your life like a coin. If you come up wounded only, you win.

Best regards

Elmo

HELEN

Mr. Cusler was at the Natural History Museum this afternoon. On Wednesday, when he came to tea, he asked if I ever visited the exhibits and I mentioned how I intended to call in while Mother was shopping with Mrs. McKeand. There he was, lurking in the Central Hall. He waved one of his crutches in the air and the crowd parted as he moved forward; people watching him, whispering their admiration. Laughing as he crossed the marble floor, performing for his audience, he gave an exaggerated swing to his crippled gait as if he intended to use his crutches to launch himself into the air. But, despite the hale athletic contortions, his eyes are deeply shadowed and there is a pale dryness to his skin which reminds me of flower petals long pressed between the pages of a book. His muscles are desperate to accelerate forward, contemptuous of their own frailty, yet he could not keep pace with the guide lecturer and so we set our own agenda, stopping three times to sit. He was grateful for the respite.

I expected someone else as the Cusler of whom Arthur writes. Someone shorter, narrower, self-effacing. Not this brash, handsome soldier. But it seems I know little of male friendship, and nothing at all of my brother. I always think of him as an adolescent, afraid to speak, his face bright with eczema. At school, he was a dull fellow, unable to throw a ball or decline a Latin verb, yet no matter what I did I could never best him. To my mother he symbolized perfection: constantly held up as the Durie saviour, the means by which we would prosper, buy back Craigluscar, restore our privilege and place.

Sometimes I walk along Spadina Road, past that elegant, pillared house, and see the people who live there now. Tradesmen. No matter how wealthy, still tradesmen; coarse, powerful, unafraid. I've known since I was a girl that Arthur couldn't save us. He possesses neither the intellect nor the will to live up to the standard set by our father. I thought education and beauty meant I could be the one. I would rise through the teaching profession to preside over an exclusive school for the daughters of the elite. I would marry into our class. But it never happened. The young men who paid court to me were entirely unsuitable. Yet I always believed tomorrow, next month, soon. Now I am not so sure.

I know why Mother has brought me to London. Arthur's wound is but one part of her concern. The army took the fittest, the tallest, the most confident, the most eligible of Englishmen and put them into officers' uniform. Every lord and duke and earl offered up their sons for the cause. The streets teem with them. And at numerous dinners and teas bored young men suggest soaring heights of heroism. I am supposed to find a husband at these gatherings, though I am a decade older than the girls who flutter around, simpering on cue. It is the elder brothers, those left behind to manage the estate, I should meet. Mother does not yet possess the connections to procure such an invitation. Next year Arthur will be working at the War Office. He will socialize with men of excellent heritage. Perhaps then it will be different.

———

Sitting on the mezzanine landing near Darwin's statue, looking across at the wall of horns – Irish elk, prehistoric bison, creatures no longer part of this earth – Mr. Cusler told me, "Bill had a difficult time when he first arrived at the front."

For a moment it was unclear as to whom he was referring. He meant Arthur. No one has ever called him Bill before – at least I think that is the case, there is much at question. I'm told Mr. Cusler is a berserker in battle, charging forward unafraid, a mythic warrior. Yet he sits at Arthur's chair, touching his arm, talking quietly, the two of them smoking cheap cigarettes despite Mother's offer of more dignified brands. I cannot fathom this friendship, this sharing.

———

He kissed me. Three times. Or perhaps just once, as I am unsure how these things are counted. At first I did not know how to respond. I thought it enough to simply accept. But he withdrew for a moment and opened my lips with his fingertip.

"Let me inside you."

Then his mouth returned to mine and his tongue drew patterns. We were standing in the hotel's parlour, Mother waiting upstairs for my return. Someone might enter at any moment. He withdrew once more. His hands ran over my shoulders and into my hair. Then more of the kiss. Images in my head: a hand turning a page, the slow spin of the ceiling fan in my grandfather's old house. A creak on the stairs, and he had left me to gaze at a watery view of Cumbria, ready to greet my mother with tales of the day and an excuse why, regrettably, tea was impossible.

He asked that I use his Christian name: Elmo. I've heard Arthur call him Ellie. It would not be correct for me to do so. He is of a family of farmers, six years younger than me, without rank or position. He said my infrequent smiles reminded him of sunlight moving over meadows. I failed to tell him of our disparities.

Dear Mrs. Durie,

I've just got your address from Lt. Ryerson and am writing to enquire about your son, Lt. Durie. We are all very anxious to know how he is getting on. When he left us we were of the impression that his wound was slight; since then we have heard that it is more serious than we thought. We are all very sorry that he got hurt and would like to know how he is getting on.

With kind regards,

D. Carmichael, Capt.

ARTHUR

When the roses bloomed I moved to a hospital in Brighton and soon was well enough to slowly walk the short block to church. At the end of that first service I stood at attention while we sang the national anthem – wheezing, clinging to the pew rail for support. There was little patriotism in my gesture: I had a point to prove to myself and to my mother. That afternoon I wrote to Colonel Genet of my wish to return and he replied with his pleasure.

In late August, Helen was to go back to Canada. I'd begun to chafe against their presence and persuaded Mother to also return and to relate her adventures to the ladies of the Canadian Red Cross. There was a suffocation in such prox-imity of family. They knew what was best for me, for my rise through the ranks and for my future. I was their cause and they were convinced of its righteousness. But I understood even then that they were wrong. In the battalion, there was finally a purpose to my life. A duty to perform. Such ideas did not remain with me. Others have evolved to take their place. But within such evolution lies my liberation.

———————

I would continue my convalescence in Scotland, in one of the many large private houses made available to the wounded. Sitting on a luggage trolley at Euston Station, my chest heaving with the exertion of our walk across the forecourt, I listened to Mother's list of all that must be done to prepare for my homecoming.

"The bank will definitely promote you in light of your service record."

Once more: "I don't intend to return to the bank."

"Nonsense, Arthur, and please do not contract your words. It sounds so common. A promotion will mean you can buy a larger house. These benefits are for Helen as well as for you. It will mean larger dinner parties, greater opportunities for you both to meet the right people."

"I will be returning to the battalion as soon as I am passed fit. That is all I can plan for at the moment."

Helen fussed with the bags, refusing to get involved.

"Well, I know you will feel differently once your convalescence is complete. If you wish to stay in the army a position in Canada could be easily obtained."

I embraced her, kissed her cheek. Even in my weakened state I could have swung her off her feet: so small and light.

So tenacious. But I no longer had the strength to argue. I'd told her too many times of my intentions. I saw no reason for further repetition.

ANNA

I can hear Helen's footsteps overhead. She is wrapping Christmas presents, pretending normality. We have left Arthur's house forever and moved into this strangeness. Helen deals with our tangled finances. I want to sleep but cannot. Neither can I eat, not even this pap the doctor ordered. My stomach will not hold. Instead I can only remember what brought me to this circumstance.

It was my father who filled my childhood with stories from every corner of the earth. Stories he knew from his father and on through the generations of New English. His family, though in Ireland for centuries, had remained ever loyal to the Church of England and English rule, and insisted on education for its scions in only the best of English schools. But they went across the world for their tales of heroes, and for myths to fire the blood. He said it was the search for roots, that an adopted child wants knowledge of all possibilities. Not so for me. My parents emigrated to New Orleans and my father prospered even more in the busy port. But I never saw the South as my home or Ireland as my heritage. My roots are planted firmly in England. The Yankees trampled the gracious southern culture; how could I possess any loyalty to America?

I was only five when my mother taught me the meaning of fidelity. Brutish, cowardly Union soldiers occupied the city, eager to loot and destroy everything that was fine. Major General Polk's wonderful library in Trinity Church, where he had served as bishop before taking up arms against the enemy, would be obliterated by those savages. It was our duty, honour, and pleasure to save his treasures. I was too small to carry any of the books but my mother said my presence was necessary and she knew I was brave enough to take part. The ladies hid the volumes beneath their hoop skirts and calmly walked from the building, attending to their children, talking lightly of dinner or of how well the clematis was blooming that year, the doltish Union soldiers oblivious to their scheme.

Mama died on board ship in the Atlantic when I was seventeen. Just Emily and me to watch over her. We had left Europe because of her illness, left my finishing school and the greatest galleries and museums in the world, and were returning to New Orleans. The captain placed her body in an unadorned coffin and told us the ceremony would be performed during the "churchyard watch" – the hours immediately after midnight – so as not to upset the passengers. In Paris I had seen the wounded of the Franco-Prussian War brought into the city on flatcars. I had not been "upset" then and I would not be now. Emily yowled and tore her hair, in such distress that the doctor repeatedly administered laudanum. It should have calmed her but it merely turned her banshee wails into mewls of sorrow. The captain had ignored my request for Mama's body to be taken home. I would show him my disdain, show him I was not a stricken girl.

I stood calmly throughout the service. It was all so brief. I remember the cold wind cutting through my shawl, the clergyman hurrying his words. I watched her slide down into the waves, barely a splash, miles to travel before she rested on the seabed.

Papa was distraught. He had no way to say goodbye. He would stand on the levee and look to the east, his lips moving to a constant stream of silent words. His stories changed: he told of Mama's beauty and her bravery. And he told us of her unconditional love for her children. He no longer spoke of the Merrow, half fish, half man, who trapped the souls of drowned sailors in lobster pots and imprisoned them forever, or of Orpheus and Eurydice or the fearlessness of Antigone. These were only myths, he told me. Reality was Mama taken from us forever. As a child I had craved all his tales, fact or fable. The lovers, the chevaliers, the Homeric deeds and fantastical truths. Gilgamesh and his friendship with the wild man Enkidu fashioned out of clay. The three Norns – Fate, Necessity, and Being – the goddesses of destiny who live beneath the giant ash tree sheltering all the worlds. Isabel and her love for Lorenzo: of how her family, thinking him unworthy, slew him. She dug his body from the earth and placed his severed head beneath a basil plant which she tended night and day. Her murderous brothers stole the pot, then, overcome by remorse, fled into exile. But still she died for want of Lorenzo.

ARTHUR

I wonder how many men are virgins at age thirty-five. After age eighteen I tried to think of my virginity as noble, as something offered to God as proof of my purity of spirit. But it was hopeless. I deluded myself only for brief moments, usually when an attractive young woman turned away from my attempts at conversation. In the privacy of my room I was as carnal as any man and then as angry, frustrated, and despairing. The girls that Mother wanted me to take an interest in were horse-faced and dull. The ones I liked were unreachable.

Mother never tired of searching for a suitable mate. Yet even those she found presentable were mentioned in half-hearted fashion. Her real enthusiasm was saved for the idyllic future in which I presented her with bouncing grandchildren conceived in an old Tudor house on an English country estate. Those two thousand acres of Surrey paradise existed for her, as real as our pocket-handkerchief garden on St. George Street in Toronto. No. More real. Other things were temporary.

"Think of it, Arthur," she would say, "arching trees, bridle paths, and hollows in which luxurious ferns grow. Stone parapets and balustrades and wide flights of shallow steps seamed by time and weather. Moss and ivy grow over them near a fountain that plays when the weather is warm."

Of course, she was remembering Craigluscar, the spacious, elegant house my father built when she was a new bride, now ratcheted up into aristocratic dimensions. My own dreams focused on the moment of conception of those grandchildren, but though I envisioned the woman and the bed and the feel of her body below me, I could never imagine how we actually got into that position or even into that bedroom. I was useless even in my fantasies.

The fact that very few nubile aristocratic girls of vast fortune actually walk the streets of Toronto bothered my mother not a jot. They would present themselves if we were patient and if we cultivated the right circle of acquaintances. Beaux for Helen were also sought. At the hospital in Étaples Mother salivated over a young lord in the next bed who perhaps had a sister of marriageable age, and over a Dorset earl with numerous siblings who had spoken to us very pleasantly on Brighton Pier one afternoon.

Girls of lesser status had little chance of discovering my charms. Helen once brought home a teacher friend from Jarvis Collegiate. It was her first year at the school. She was extremely pretty, wearing a wide-brimmed and very fetching lavender-coloured hat. I found the young woman sitting patiently on the porch when I came home from the bank. She was waiting for Helen to finish dressing. So I talked to her. Or rather she talked to me. She was happy that her brother had just been accepted into university, that her father's illness had passed, that the autumn colours were perfect, that her pupils at Jarvis were doing remarkably well, that my job was so interesting. I felt happy too. I wanted to discover how it came about that she seemed to be lingering there just for me. Then the car arrived for them both and we said our goodbyes. The next day at breakfast I asked about her. In the evening Mother made known her views.

"A woman such as she could not understand anything about you, Arthur. Her thoughts are those of a lower order of being who knows nothing of art, literature, or learning. Nothing noble, nothing refining, ever came out of her class."

The young woman never visited again.

Ironically, when the time finally came, at thirty-five years and five months, I lost my virginity to a bona fide aristocrat, but my mother can never know. First because it's none of her business, and also because it was not of her world. It was real love, for both of us. I believe that sincerely. Love does not have to be the way Mother describes it. It isn't necessarily a lifetime of devotion, before and after the grave; it doesn't need portraits over the mantel or even promises of faithfulness. It can add up to no more than a few hours. But that slice of time, whatever circumstance permits, is as valid and as perfect as any ceremony before God or State.

I met her at Wemyss Castle, an ancient heap perched on cliffs overlooking the wild seas of Scotland. No, I'm not hallucinating. It was a Tuesday, surely a prosaic day, and I was struggling to understand the cab driver's thick Scottish accent, but his voice rose as his frustration grew, and that did not help. I must have looked alarmed, my usual expression when I'm trying to cope with the unexpected; my lung ached and my breath began to labour. Suddenly she was there, the man doffing his cap, and she knew my name, told me tales as she led me through endless rooms. At some point she must have introduced herself as Lady Eva Wemyss, I don't recall the moment. She explained turnpike stairs and murder holes, and conspiracies and romance, and I was in the centre of a conversation I didn't know had even begun before I remembered I hadn't paid the cab fare. And I was at ease.

"Mary Queen of Scots first laid eyes on Lord Darnley right here on St. Valentine's Day, 1565," she said as we crossed the old gallery. "Mary said he was 'the properest and best proportioned long man that ever she had seen.'" I knew Mary's story. An ancestor of mine, George Durie, was abbot of

Dunfermline during her reign. In fact, the old Durie lands lie on the east side of the River Leven, directly across the water from the Wemyss estate.

"He was very, very handsome. But he was also vain, dissipated, and vicious. He was dancing at that first sighting. If a man can dance he can hide a great many flaws."

"Not for long," I replied. "Within a year she plotted his murder."

"No, I don't agree, Mr. Durie. I think she was guilty of a great many things but not of that. She lost control of her destiny. Other people with their own ambitions took over her life."

———————

Hundreds of people in Great Britain have opened their stately homes and country houses to the wounded and given soldiers some respite from the mayhem. Wemyss Castle took in eight officers at a time and I have no idea how those eight were chosen. But it is strange indeed that a Canadian soldier was selected to convalesce in an area imprinted with his ancestors.

The castle has been home to the Wemyss family for five hundred years. Lady Eva, widow of the late laird, Randolph, is its mistress. In the three weeks I was there, her brother-in-law Hugo Wemyss was also in residence. But most of the Wemyss clan would not dream of visiting. Eva had been the "other woman," the cause of her husband's divorce from his first wife, the cause of the rift with his children and with most of the remaining family. Randolph was a man of passion and impulse and restless energy who died only ten years after his second marriage. But he continued to spit out rancour from his grave. He left a will expressly forbidding his first wife or any of her family *ever* to reside at the castle. The bad blood boiled and Eva was ostracized, left alone to conduct her charitable works in the small coal town, to supervise the running of the castle as a convalescent home, to walk the clifftops. She never spoke of these trials to me. It was Hugo who described her loneliness. In the mornings she joined us officers for breakfast: coffee, a little kedgeree, that was all. We were a retiring octet. Each man solitary in his habits, completing his limping, wheezing, scarred recuperation. At the dinner hour she inquired after the day's events, whether letters brought news of a child's whooping cough or told if family roses survived the greenfly infestation. She spoke least of all to me. I thought it significant.

After only two days of Scottish exercise I knew the hills were too challenging for my crippled lung, so I took my daily walks along the cliffs or over the beach, feeling the air push into my lopsided chest. One day, as I tramped the seashore, watching the villagers dig for rag worms, then fish over the seabed, I heard a shout, and Eva ran across the packed sand. Women over the age of eighteen rarely run, a sort of accelerated swish is the norm. She ran. Scattering the seabirds. Sending divots of sand hurtling from her heels. Her face was flushed, her dark hair escaping from its pins. We walked together and I began to tell her something of my affinity with this place, the ancestors who had long strolled this same beach. She listened without comment until I had exhausted the queen's favourite, and the abbot, and the Durie who came over with William the Conqueror.

"It is fascinating to think who we used to be," she said, "and to contemplate how easily our fortunes change, yet how long we carry their legacy."

I thought of Aeneas, escaping from Troy with his father on his back. He felt so much love for the old man but was weighed down by the duty it required. I didn't ask about Eva's history or about her marriage and her own particular fortunes. I wanted her only in the present, walking with me.

She told me the story of Hardy's *Tess of the D'Urbervilles*, the pure peasant girl whose destruction begins when her wastrel father learns of the family's noble lineage. I read the book on the train journey south.

"'There's not a man in the county of South Wessex that's got grander and nobler skillentons in his family than I.'"

I laughed, though I already knew the sadness in John Durbeyfield's statement, how he had been seduced by the idea of his own importance. I'd thought of it for a long time after the conversation on the beach. My own family is convinced of its social superiority, the pure knowledge of our aristocratic grandeur – ensconced in a semi-detached house. Despite the precious family documents we harbour, we are not Duries "of that ilk," as the Scots describe it. Not Duries of Durie. We are some distant branch, an afterthought, as much removed from the upper classes as any officer at the Wemyss breakfast table.

The world does not have the order accorded it by my mother and deviation from such an imagining is not anarchy. Instead the world is a wondrous place of fascinating twists and turns, and a place of egalitarian evil.

"Perhaps you would like to see the dungeons, Mr. Durie. There is much history in the house."

I wanted to spend time with her, any time; time with her quiet assurance. She calmed me.

———

The electricity did not reach those deep rooms, and lanterns were necessary to show the way. Eva led, the flame trickling along her shoulder and into the soft folds of fabric. The long zigzag passageway swallowed the light, so she seemed like a firefly that silently appeared and disappeared. It was cold and the smell of the sea was strong. I asked no questions, had no wish to find out exactly what happened there, why such a place was necessary. Pinching – that's what they called the gentlest pressure used. No food or water sent into the dank space, only moisture dripping from the roof to sustain the prisoner and so "pinch" his body into submission. In the egg-shaped chamber, rusted iron hooks oozed from the walls. Once, iron gauntlets hung from them, and a man, dangling for hours.

I remembered an image in a school book: Guy Fawkes's signature before and after torture. A firm hand falling into an agonized jerk of ink. For him it took less than a day. Wrists and ankles attached to rollers by sturdy ropes, levers turning, dislocating the shoulders, pulling the femur from the hip. Broken, in a room such as this. They displayed him in public. Utterly broken. A warning to all.

I used to struggle to learn the dates, the order of kings, the parliamentary pronouncements, and never could recall the names of battles or of ministers. But I always understood the people on the page and could identify their terrors: Henry Hudson's son tied like a dog outside an Eskimo igloo, Christopher Marlowe fighting for his life in a tavern, Guy

Fawkes feeling his beliefs ripped away with every creak of the lever. It is impossible to conjure up pain, to realize how it will consume everything. How there will be no will, no coherence, only its presence. I knew pain had taken residence in that room. There were no ghosts there to haunt me and no pall of evil engulfing me or good spirits to show the way to enlightenment. Nothing so fanciful. Instead those walls had absorbed the totality of torment. Every agony of torn flesh gathered in the corners, took sustenance, and grew, until pain was in possession, was palpable. I tried to breathe calmly, carefully, so it wouldn't know my history, wouldn't recognize its own power. But it heard the slight rasp of my lung echoing in that damp room and its fingers searched out the scar tissue that refused to heal, and began to squeeze. I was in the dugout again. The air refusing to sustain me. Discomfort, suffering, turning into waves of torment, unable to focus, cold stone against my back as my legs began to buckle. Fire consumed my chest. Terror of dying underground, of the rats that would swarm from the stones and gnaw on my living flesh. Then the pressure of her hand on my wrist and she was pulling, tugging, forcing me to follow, dragging me along the crenellations of the trench, until she shoved violently against my shoulders and, as my heels met resistance, I stumbled backward to sit hard upon the steps.

Free of that room, my pain was abating. I could hear her voice though not yet recognize the words. Something soothing. And I could feel her hand, now holding not my wrist but my long narrow fingers. I felt no embarrassment. She understood. Just as she understood those stairs were my sanctuary, where to regain my composure and learn to breathe again.

Away from that hideous place but not yet under the curious eyes of staff or guests. She waited until I was calm, all the time watching me. Then she lent forward and kissed my lips, a soft, scented pressure. My eyes were open. I had never been kissed. She withdrew a fraction and raised her head just a little so that her lips brushed my moustache, lifting it, tickling it. She smiled. Her tongue snaked out and licked around my mouth so it opened, ready to receive her breath. She dipped into the well, gliding along my teeth. My own tongue met hers and she lapped over its surface. My fingers curled into the satin of her hair.

"Tomorrow," she said, "we will take a drive. You should see more of the country your family once owned."

Telegraph} "Thane"
Address} Kirkcaldy
Telephone} No. 4 Dysart.
Wemyss Castle
Fife
Sunday, September 17th 1916.

My dearest Helen,
I have not written to you and Mother for nearly a week. I have received all your letters; August 28th and one from New York September 1st, also Mother's of August 29th and September 1st, and was so glad to hear from both of you that you had had a good

voyage across and had arrived safely in Toronto. In my last letter I forgot to tell you I had received your cable.

I came up here from London last Tuesday, journeying by day, and it was very pretty coming through the country. I am in a lovely place here belonging to Lady Eva Wemyss. It is a very large estate near Kirkcaldy and not very far from Dunfermline and near Leven. The castle is simply beautiful, right down by the sea, and very old, and there is a chapel. Besides Lady Eva Wemyss there are Mr Hugo Wemyss and Miss Wemyss, relations who are visiting here. Lady Eva is a dear and has been exceptionally kind to me. Durie is near Leven, which is very near here, and I think I shall walk over and see it. Is it not a very curious thing that I should have come to the place to which we used to belong? There is a Mr. G—— here who lives on the estate and is very old. He asked me to go and see him, which I did, and he was very nice indeed. He had a whole lot of notes about our family and he also had a commission of Robert Durie's dated 1600.

Wemyss Castle is a beautiful, old place overlooking the North Sea. When I crossed the Forth Bridge yesterday I saw the Fleet, and I also saw some of the battle ships steaming out to sea.

I do want my civilian clothes very much and I am expecting them shortly. Miss M—— will send them as soon as they arrive. Well, dearest Helen, I think I have told you all the news I have and I shall write very soon again. By-the-by, I have received a letter from Mr. R—— and one from Mrs. B—— and will answer both of them.

With all the love I have for yourself and dearest Mother, Your affectionate brother,

Arthur

ARTHUR

Eva drove. She had dismissed the chauffeur, telling him to share the day with his wife instead. We spent hours travelling the braes through driving rain, occasionally sprinting to some ruined pile or historic plaque to discover its provenance. I'd borrowed rubber boots and a long mackintosh from the castle; our bodies were dry but the rain dripped from our noses. We ate a picnic in the car peering out across the firth, rarely speaking but entirely comfortable in the silence.

There was only a misty dampness remaining in the air by the time we passed along the edge of Loch Leven. The loch's water level was low and the exposed mud was a feeding ground for hundreds and hundreds of birds. Eva knew them all: the golden plover, the curlew, the exact species of swan swooping above the water. We stepped from the car but ventured only a few yards forward.

"Some winter nights the geese fly under the full moon," she said. "It is a rare and beautiful thing to see."

The wind blew from the land and I stood behind her as a shelter from the chill. As she spoke she leaned into me until I was holding her weight and her spine curved along my chest. "Randolph and I came here so many times and only once did we see the night flight. There must be a thin veil of cloud to silhouette the birds against the sky and the full moon must rise a few hours after sunset so the geese have time to roost and rest before the light persuades them to go again in search of food. We sat on these banks, quiet and still, and listened as the clamouring grew louder and louder. Much louder than we'd ever heard before. As if they were all arguing the feasibility of their plans. Then for a few seconds there was total silence and I could see Randolph's eyes sparkling in anticipation. And suddenly, in one huge whoosh, they took to the air, thousands upon thousands of them passing under the moon."

She shivered with the memory. I could pretend it was the chill and offer my jacket, suggest we leave, gently take her elbow and guide her into the motor. But the edicts that were always my sanctuary in the presence of women, the rules of etiquette so carefully adhered to, seemed pointless. I wrapped my arms around her.

Across the loch stood the grim fortress where the renegade nobles imprisoned Mary. They had gathered under a banner portraying Darnley's corpse and the motto "Judge and avenge my cause, oh Lord." Mary was tricked and captured. In clothes caked with mud, the beautiful queen was paraded through the crowd and its obscene jeers. "Burn the whore, kill her, drown her." They brought her to this loneliness.

"I want to go home, Bill."

"So do I," I answered.

I felt her smile.

———

That night, in my room, I dressed and undressed a half dozen times. Slippers, pyjamas, robe; full uniform; jacket and tie removed; trousers and undershirt; pyjamas only. Finally, just the robe. Sitting upon a straight-backed chair, I waited. We had said nothing of this on the journey home but I knew she would come to me. Telling the story makes it sound like a schoolboy quivering outside the headmaster's office. Perhaps so. Everything in me prickled with joy yet there was an undercurrent of fear. What if I made a total fool of myself? The procedure was foreign to me, known only from bawdy jokes, army health pamphlets, and the distant memory of incoherent narratives told on the way home from school. I knew the texture of my own flesh, but images of how a woman would feel or react only jelled into glowing Titian figures or dispassionate Carrara marble. What if she expected something of which I hadn't the faintest notion: practices, common practices, entirely unknown to me? What would Cusler do in these circumstances – the master of seduction? I had no idea. And after trying to conjure his voice, coaching me, I realized it wasn't a matter of preliminaries, not a case of devising how my desire could merge into action. That part was already accomplished. I'd read it in the way her body melted into mine at Loch Leven, like a bank colleague's infant child I once held. A boneless moulding of flesh. Rather, would years of self-abuse cause my cock to malfunction? Perhaps I wouldn't get hard, wouldn't come, wouldn't stop coming, would sputter and stammer and fill her body with my inadequacies. There was a young private of my company who tagged along with his friends on a visit to a brothel in Poperhinghe only a short time after we first arrived in Belgium. He attempted to tie the poor girl's feet together in the same way he'd hobble the farm mares back home before fucking them. Her shouts of protest brought in the madam, who ejected every Canadian, without a refund, no matter what company or battalion. The boy would still be listening to his comrades' ribald jokes and insults if he hadn't been eviscerated a month later.

I could hear the rumbles of the sea. In the moonlight the thistles, roses, and fleurs-de-lys of the frieze glistened above me. I wanted to see her, examine everything, but knew I must not turn on the electric light. She would discern my fear. I was an amalgam of terror and arousal, stomach churning. Suddenly she was silently there. Standing before my chair she lifted her nightgown so her whiteness grew from the floor like a slow Roman candle. Unspeaking, she straddled my lap and in one movement slid onto me, grinding damp heat around my balls. My hands found the weight of her breasts and I felt her muscles clench around my shaft. Her fingers reached down and began to move against herself. The sudden shock of ripples drew my own orgasm from me in a white-hot squall. Some guttural cry escaped my throat. Panic began to well. I didn't want it to be over so soon. But she held my face, quietened me. Told me she wanted more. She leaned across to switch on the table lamp and I watched the wonder of her nakedness as her hips started to rock, ever so slightly. She began to teach me how.

If asked to recount every moment of that night, I could. There is nothing lost to me. But as time passes, my main recollection is not of orgasm or intensity. Instead I see her lying next to me, my arm across her body, my hand cupping her breast in ownership. I did own her that night and every night at Wemyss. As she owned me.

She came to me each evening, in frenzied need or in slow exploration. She taught me all the variations of a kiss. She controlled me and allowed herself to be controlled. She asked to watch me shave and sat naked on the edge of the chair as I stood similarly naked at the mirror. She wanted to see me bathe but I didn't possess the patience. Instead I took her hand and led her to the bed. We made love. I drank my seed from her body and kissed it into her waiting mouth. Love. Perfect and entire unto itself. Contained within a room in an ancient castle. It was enough.

On the last morning she sat cross-legged in the dawn light watching intently as I dressed.

"Why are you staring?"

"Because I will never see this again."

She was telling only the truth. I stood over her one last time and bent to her kiss. The angle of her naked body folded onto the bed meant she could touch nothing except my lips. She was unable to wrap her arms, her legs, around mine and I denied her the touch of my skin. I could feel all her cravings sliding up from her torso into that final goodbye.

She did not appear at breakfast. I made small talk with each of the officers. Then I left the table and began my journey back to the mud.

ANNA

One-third of the inhabitants of New Orleans departed the city each summer. Wishing to avoid heat, disease, and hurricane, they left the streets empty except for hearses on their way to the Cities of the Dead.

My father always sent us to his cousin Dr. Reid's home in the village of Thornhill in southern Ontario. And that is where I first met Lieutenant-Colonel William Smith Durie, deputy adjutant-general for the 2nd Military District. He had been conducting a militia review in the neighbourhood, his bearing so upright, confident, and authoritative in the splendid frogged uniform and cocked hat with fine white plume. Famed as the first commanding officer of the Queen's Own Rifles, he captivated me. His family held property in the area, and from then on, I would watch him – at summer gatherings, at dinner parties, on his walks along the banks of the Don.

I knew his pedigree was impeccable, and Dr. Reid filled in the details of the family's lineage. The Duries were warriors, entering Britain with William the Conqueror. They were administrators to Henry II's sister Princess Joan, who married a king of Scotland. One was a provost of Dunfermline; one so skilled in medicine that she saved the life of Charles I after the physicians had despaired; one a prelate and statesman whose loyalty to Mary Queen of Scots gave him a reputation for devotion such as few men ever enjoyed.

William's aristocratic breeding ensured he was never overbearing despite his obvious superiority. He was always polite, showed ill will to no man, and made light of his own favours. He was of brilliant mind and had an immediate grasp of politics and diplomacy, and as he watched how the world unfolded he recognized danger in the rise of the middle class.

"I consider their feelings," I once heard him say to Dr. Reid, "while they have no hesitation in speaking their minds regardless of my sensibilities. They consciously like doing it. The universities are responsible. The seats of learning are turning out hundreds of men without education in the truest sense of the word, enabling them to enter professions for which they have no real qualifications. A man must be able to go back hundreds of years in tracing his fine qualities."

I listened. And I saw him become aware of my listening.

His position as deputy adjutant-general based him at Fort York in Toronto. The coach journey took three hours yet his visits grew more frequent and soon his stories were told only to me.

He asked for my hand. I was twenty-one. He was sixty-four. The age difference was meaningless, no matter what jealous gossip circulated in the village. I was privileged to be chosen as wife to such a man.

———

Work began on our home, Craigluscar, named for the old Durie estate in Scotland. It was to be a handsome house, in spacious grounds overlooking the city. As a girl, I'd lived for three years in Paris, Brussels, Dresden, and Leipzig. I'd studied painting and music and visited the great galleries and opera houses. I knew life in Toronto would be arid after my experiences in the cultural heart of the world. But no sacrifice was too great in exchange for the Durie name. And I wanted William.

Young men in New Orleans had stolen kisses, dry loose pressings that gave no pleasure. But William taught me of a man's passion. I would lie with Emily in the darkness of our bedroom and remember his embraces. Tell her of the sensations they caused. Poor Emily never married, was never kissed, she lived only through me. Once, in New Orleans, our carriage stopped while a brewer's wagon turned in the narrow street. Father leaned from the window and berated the driver for choosing such a route through this unsavoury part of town, while we girls stared open-mouthed down a narrow alleyway as a tall man in a fashionable plaid suit thrust against a young woman's dishevelled pale blue satin. His tall-crowned bowler lay neatly on the sidewalk. I could see the stark white skin of the woman's limbs, her fingers clenching into the fabric of his jacket sleeve. The gentleman's head was thrown back, his eyes tight closed and his face holding the rictus of a silent scream. I was horrified, frightened at the blatant intensity. Then suddenly the way was clear, the carriage moved on. And I was left to wonder how it would be to cause a man such harrowing pleasure.

One Sunday afternoon, as I walked in the garden with William, he asked if I knew anything of the physical aspects of marriage. I felt my cheeks burn, and told him I would certainly do as was my duty. He hesitated, and his manner puzzled me. Then, in full view of the porch where Dr. Reid read his newspaper, William explained it was not duty he wanted from his bride, it was pleasure, his and hers. He said he wished to teach me about love between a man and a woman. He said that in Scotland a couple who consummated their relationship after betrothal were considered to be married. The Church of Scotland saw such a marriage as legal. And, of course, an aristocratic betrothal held its own canon.

With Emily as our designated chaperone, the arrangements were easy. What surprised me was my pleasure. His whiskers moved across my skin. He twisted and turned my body as if I were the weight of a blossom. My pregnancy was not the result of some hurried furtive coupling. William was my lover. I have no regrets. Beneath his hands I became alive. I was his warrior, his consort, his love. He taught me who I am.

First Casualty Training
Battalion, Canadians
Shoreham on Sea,
Monday, November 20th 1916

My dearest Mother,

I received your cable last night, and was very surprised. I do not want a job, and was very sorry you spoke to Sir Sam Hughes. I could have got some sort of a job in London, but would rather rejoin the 58th. Please do not say anything more about it. Everyone knows I want to go back and I am afraid you have only done me harm, because your cable was telephoned to the Adjutant here. I know dearest Mother, you think you do things for the best, but don't you think you are sometimes a little impetuous. This is a Battalion where all the officers and men return to their own Battalion in France, and I will rejoin the 58th in due course.

I have not yet heard who is to be the new Minister of Militia. I do not think it will be Sir George Perley. Just take things quietly, as I am doing, and everything will be all right.

We are moving to Hastings tomorrow, and I will write you immediately on my arrival there.

With all the love I have for yourself and dearest Helen.

Your affectionate son,

Arthur

ARTHUR

What was she thinking? Despite my express wishes my mother travelled to Ottawa to meet with Sir Sam Hughes. It isn't easy to obtain an interview with the minister of militia and defence at a time of war. Especially one who is in open conflict with his prime minister and has just been asked to resign.

Seated in Hughes's office on Parliament Hill, she spoke about my father's service to his country, about how his work in shaping the Queen's Own Rifles echoed down into the making of the Canadian army. She listed Durie achievements and honours and included my wound and my work in the 58th. Sir Sam, a militiaman since the time of the Fenian raids and well familiar with my father's work, agreed, saying it was a small thing indeed considering how much the Duries had given. He promised a Staff position immediately. He is well known for his patronage appointments and perhaps approved a whole slew of them in his final days, but surely he also said yes just to get this tenacious woman away from his desk.

I knew nothing of these matters until a cable arrived at the training battalion in England, just days before I was due to leave for the front. It took a great deal of explaining to put matters right. And it took a great deal of restraint to tell my mother of my refusal.

No matter what I say her efforts are unceasing. Hughes's resignation was not a problem: she simply cultivated a friendship with his successor, Edward Kemp. A few months later word came through of yet another Staff appointment, as town major in Maroc, responsible for billeting arrangements far behind the lines. I'd never applied for such a position! Not even discussed the possibility. I asked the brass to cancel it immediately, said that under no circumstances would I take up the appointment. There ensued a great flurry of messages back and forth and with them murmurs of insubordination. Colonel Genet eventually sent a letter explaining the situation, but he would not let me see what he wrote. I know something about my mother's interference was in there. I'm sure there was much laughter at HQ.

Other battalion officers are wounded and then return. It is what we do – though each has his own reasons as to why it is necessary, why we must continue the cycle. Do they recognize my loneliness? Do they see how I hide within the chaos?

First Casualty Training
Battalion, Canadians
Hastings, December 4th, 1916
Monday, 2.30 P.M.

My dearest Mother,
I have not received letters from you or Helen for two weeks. As I told you we are in billets, that is in empty houses. We have to walk about half a mile for our meals, up to Battalion Headquarters. I have just rented a bed, which is a very great comfort. The meals are not good; but I have gone down once or twice to an hotel in Hastings for dinner. My right lung is in fairly good condition; not exactly as it was before; but it is pulling very well. The country

round about is hilly and I breathe a little heavily when I climb some of the hills; that is the only thing that affects me, and that not very badly. The division Headquarters have asked twice for a list of officers fit for service. They asked again last Saturday, and I think some of us will be evacuated very soon. I have been with this Battalion three weeks today, and there are not many officers who were here before me, so I may be warned. If I am I will cable you immediately, but they would probably give me two or four days leave at once. The weather for the last day or two has been cold and fairly dry. Captain and Mrs. McKeand have, I think, gone back to Canada. Colonel Genet is still with the 58th and Alex Macfarlane is Second in Command. I do not know where Captain Cosbie is, but he is still alive.

I have met a number of the 58th men here. A good many of them are in the Canadian Casualty Assembly Centre. Nearly all of them have given me the cheerful news that I was dead; indeed I think that rumour was fairly well believed by the men. One of them told me someone had got my picture out of a Toronto paper and pinned it up in the front lines with the words: "Good old Durie"; so I was supposed to have left this happy world for a better one — or worse. If I should go back it will be to the 58th; all officers leaving here return to their own Battalions. If I do not go in the next draft I shall probably be a month or more in England. The 58th, as far as I know, is in a pretty good part of the line now, probably taking a well-needed rest. Colonel Genet, I think, is soon coming back to England for good. Someone told me that Captain McNair was shot through the body, and knowing he was mortally wounded, he took out his wife's picture and looked at it. A German saw him and finished him with a bullet through the head. I feel sure this is true.

Last Saturday I went out to Battle to see the place the battle of Hastings was fought. There is an abbey there, built on the old Saxon lines. I saw the place where William the Conqueror lowered the Saxon colours, the spot where Harold is supposed to have been killed and the hill over which the Normans charged. Battle is about five miles inland from the sea, and I always thought the battle of Hastings was fought right down by the sea; but that is not the case. The whole place is extremely interesting. There is nothing to see in Hastings; it is very uninteresting and very hilly but with quite a long water front. We are billeted a little out of the town, about twenty minutes ride in the tram. I am going up to London very soon. I should think if I go over all letters would be forwarded to me; the address will be 58th Battalion, 9th Brigade, 3rd Division, Canadians, France. I have put this down in case you have forgotten it. I should think officers would be kept at the base in France for a few days or for a week; but I am not sure about this. If I should be going over and should get four days leave, I will go to the hotel at once. I cannot think of any more news.

With all the love I have for yourself and dearest Helen,

Your affectionate son,

W. A. P. Durie.

ARTHUR

In the days of long ago, when men of courage were plentiful in the land, lived Fionn mac Cumhail. He could swim through the waves like a dolphin and was faster than the sparrows; water from his cupped hand gave life to the dying. He was a warrior, a seer, and commander-in-chief of the Fianna of Erin, the ragtag warriors to whom he taught honour and duty and loyalty to one's comrades above all things. Fionn's beloved son, Oisín, fell in love with Niamh, daughter of the king of the Land of Youth, and she in turn fell in love with his wisdom and his valour and his sword-blue eyes. She took him away to the island of Tír na nÓg, "delightful is the land beyond all dreams." Oisín was happy there but after a year he wished to visit his friends and family. Niamh presented him with a white fairy steed that could gallop over water, and warned him never to set his own foot upon the earth. He kissed her goodbye and rode like the spring breezes to his cherished homeland, anxious to feel the love of his kinfolk once again, but instead of his father's Great Hall and fine white houses he found only mounds of earth and the wind blowing through the gorse bushes. Instead of a tall strong people he found only tired, shrunken men weighed down by care and in awe of this golden-haired stranger.

In one of the impoverished fields Oisín came upon a group of puny mortals trying in vain to move a giant boulder so they might till the land. Oisín leaned from his horse and his fingertips rolled the stone away without effort. But the girth of the saddle broke and he tumbled to the earth. As his body splayed upon the ground, his fine clothes turned to dun, his skin sagged and wrinkled, his limbs grew feeble and his eyes blind. Three hundred years, not one, had passed since Oisín left his comrades to dwell in the Land of Youth. And all was changed.

———

I was back in the lines for less than two weeks. I thought I was ready. Not quite hardened, but otherwise fine. But I was a different man to when I had left and I was in a different place. The rain was so heavy it caused trenches and dugouts to cave in. Walking along the duckboards, thigh deep in freezing water, was bad, but walking to the saps was much worse. The hunched slog into no man's land traversed a link between front line and listening post no deeper than a shallow ditch, and if there ever had been duckboards laid down they'd long ago disappeared into the slime. Each step was . . . no, there were no steps. Each was a drag through that sludge, a push against the mass of it, the struggle to force muscle through an opposing will. My heart thundered with the effort of forward motion. A score of times my breath fled my lungs and refused to return. I would hold my knees and draw in air an ounce at a time, wheezing like a dotard. It took forty-five minutes for me to reach the hole in which some poor man crouched. I never tried to rally him, didn't attempt any words of patriotic fervour. I simply took his report in exchange for a handful of aniseed balls. Mother sends the supply and I always decant them into a small tobacco tin so they fit easily into my tunic. They carry an interesting hint of Bulwark cut plug. I'd watch the man's eyes scrunch at the sweetness and his mouth suck to find the unfolding tang of aniseed. A remembrance of pleasure. Those men: filth-encrusted, alone in the night, spread-eagled so the mud would bear them up.

Private George Thorn took his turn out there in the darkness with orders to be back at the front line by six a.m. On the Wednesday morning he didn't arrive. Perhaps the mud engulfed him, perhaps he fell asleep, perhaps a German soldier had quietly ended his watch. I stared through the periscope as the sun rose, willing him to appear and safely claim his rum ration. He was of my platoon, my responsibility. I didn't know him well; he'd been part of a reinforcing draft that arrived in my absence. But he was around my age, and when I visited him in the sap the soft burr of his Gloucestershire birthplace was a balm to my aching lungs. Then suddenly there he was, weaving across the terrain, clearly visible in the dawn light. The night's dusting of snow perfectly silhouetted his khaki. There was no rifle fire from the Germans and neither was there a sound from our trenches, but both sides had seen him. I knew why the Hun was silent. Right at that moment a sniper, probably more than one, was beading Thorn perfectly in his sights. It would be an easy shot, slow and lazy, a practice to start the day. Thorn was puffing, his breath making clouds in the morning air. They allowed him to get so close. Four more steps. Three more. Then a single crack and he fell, his arms reaching toward the parapet. Four men immediately jumped the bags and dragged him into the trench. No more shots. The sniper probably went to have his breakfast, satisfied with such an early success.

The bullet had entered the neck, and blood arced gracefully into the air. A sergeant pressed his hands tight against the broken flesh. The flow simply diverted into myriad streams. Thorn was staring at me.

"Mum. Help me, Mum." The words low, pleading.

I knelt, frozen, in the red mud as his fingers plucked at my uniform.

"Mum, please. Please, Mum." Tears welled in his eyes.

Should I have offered a sham maternal love? I don't know. Maybe I would have bewildered him. Or brought great comfort. Everything here is second-guessing. How can I possibly know what to do in this place? I was impotent, his blood pooling at my knees. I stroked his brow and said the Lord's Prayer low against his ear.

———

Comrades stitched his body into a blanket and, hours later, under cover of darkness, trundled it along the old French military tramway to the Ecoivres cemetery. Wooden crosses stretched into the night, a chronology of the war. Over a thousand Frenchmen lie there; then come the graves of the North Midlanders, who took over the line in March 1916; the 25th Division, who died in May; the 47th Londoners, who lasted from July to October. Next it was our turn. The Canadian dead were numerous then. Now? I haven't counted.

I clasped my hands in prayer as I stood at the grave, more expedient than pious. I was shaking. A tremor refusing to depart. I could still feel Thorn's brow beneath my hand. Hot, a testament to his flight across no man's land. Moist with sweat. A thousand pieces of grit rolled across the pads of my fingers. His baby-fine hair ghosting across my knuckles in the cemetery's slight breeze.

The shaking wouldn't stop. I couldn't hold a cup without spilling half its contents. I couldn't write without dragging a spider trail across the page. Ironic. The only subject in which I'd excelled at school was penmanship. For the first days I tried to hide it, clutching my hands behind my back or folding them under my armpits. But Thorn's fevered brow wouldn't leave me be.

———————

Days passed and it took more and more effort to pull my body through the mire. Trench walls were collapsing on top of the men, whole structures crumbled under the onslaught of yet more rain. And through it the tremors grew worse and became something else entirely; my hand, into my arm, along my shoulder. Like a dog shaking the lake water from its fur. I was an old man: palsied, rasping, pathetic. On Christmas Day, Colonel Genet told me Central Training Camp at Le Havre had requested a temporary officer and he felt I'd be the best for the job. We both knew it was nonsense.

Genet watches over his men. He understands a soul's limitations, perhaps because he has studied his own. He took leave during Vimy. Has reported "sick" immediately before planned carnage. Would go on more leave prior to Passchendaele. Now he has gone for good. He was fifty-three, racked with rheumatism. He saw the things I saw. He was brave for a while. I cannot fault him.

I lasted two weeks at Le Havre. Private Thorn visited me each night. He would lie beside me on the bed and pull my hand to his forehead. His blood spurted onto my pillow and seeped along the mattress. I wanted to change the past, wanted to pretend for him, to offer him a mother's comfort. And I wanted to apologize, so badly. He was my responsibility, and I'd failed him. Surely I could tell him. But I was trapped in the congealing blood, locked in place, dumb. My throat produced gurgles and rasps as I tried to force the sounds into words. The only movement was in my hand, stroking across his brow.

Those at training camp decided a constantly weeping officer with violent shakes was not the best greeting for raw troops. I was forwarded on to a convalescent home and diagnosed with neurasthenia . . . shell shock.

Hotel Belle Vue
Menton
February 1st, 1917

My dearest Helen,
I cannot tell you the indescribable beauty of this place! I pinch myself to find out whether I am waking or sleeping. In front of me, within a stone's throw, the Mediterranean and Italy a point on the left; Monte-Carlo which I passed yesterday, the last station on the line of railway.

Arthur was standing on the platform to meet me as the train pulled in. I did not really expect him, because there had been difficulty in getting out my telegram from Paris, to say that I was coming. When I sent the telegram I had my passport with me, and that apparently settled the matter, for there he was in the flesh. He was extremely hoarse and has a bad bronchial cough; but it is really not his lungs. He feels now that it was rather a mistake to have gone into the trenches so soon. He has really been put back six months and they will never pass him here for the front; although it puts them in a difficult position when he insists on being passed, the inference being that he can benefit himself by going.

He says everything is very grim at the front and different, and he made me ill by telling me about one of his men who was killed just beside him. There was no shelling, but snipers all the time. Once a sausage dropped so near him that a clod of earth struck him on the shoulder. He thought he had been hit and gave himself up for lost. Just now he has a shattered look; but I feel sure he will be better before long.

This afternoon I went to Monte-Carlo. You can hardly imagine how extraordinary it was to be really in the Casino. No British officer is allowed to enter the gaming room. If he did he would at once be placed under arrest. I went in alone, and I cannot describe my sensations as I watched the play. "This cannot be I", was all I could think. I could not make head or tail of the play; but the Bank was winning; for when the public is winning they ring a bell. The wheel is set in the centre of a large table with figures in squares at either end. The people seated at the table place what appeared to be ivory discs with numbers at the intersections of the squares. In almost every case the croupier raked the ivory discs in as soon as the wheel stopped. I saw a number of very fashionably dressed women at the Casino; but the women at the tables did not appear to be rich women. Most of the hotels here are closed, dozens of them huge buildings behind palms with all the windows shuttered. The Casino is a wonderful place; but I will send you some picture post-cards. I could write on all night about the beauties of the place. This is just the beginning of the Alps, so the mountains are not high. At the foot of the range there is the street and promenade and every-thing else is on the mountain side. The path to this hotel, "the zig-zag" winds backward and forward to reach the level of the building.

It is a lovely place. Arthur insisted on my coming here and I must say it is very pleasant.

The crossing to Havre was rough and not very comfortable. The work of showing our passports was interminable. I had only a few minutes to catch my train for Paris and had to leave Miss U——, the American, behind. She had a trunk, which had to be examined, and they literally held her up over her passport. If I tell you about Paris I shall keep on writing all night. I drove at once in a taxi from the Gare St. Lazare to the Gare de Lyon, apparently across Paris, for we drove for ages along the Rue d'Opéra. It really was quite wonderful to be there. After I had had my luncheon I sallied forth and took a tram marked "Louvre." This took me to the Louvre and I made my way to the Tuileries and on down to the Place de la Concorde and Champs Elysees. Strange to say Arthur did much the same thing. He says Paris is the most beautiful city in the world. I feel it the most awful shame that you are not with me; but I am not sure that you could have borne the strain of trying to get over. It was _fierce_ and required a vast amount of patience. After my passport had been viséed by the French Consulate, the Foreign Office, Downing Street, told me practically that I could not go, and I talked as I never talked before and won out. When I left London I felt as if I had been ground to powder. They tell me I shall have difficulty getting back, but I don't believe it. I arrived in Paris about one o'clock and left at eight. After my voyage of discovery, I returned to the Gare de Lyon about five, for Paris is dark at night though not as dark as London.

The cable we got from Arthur that memorable Sunday morning was censored out of recognition. It should have read: "Leaving for France Monday." Arthur received all our Christmas parcels but nothing from Alice. In the end he will get her things, so I should not tell her, it is so dreadfully disappointing. He ate my cake and candies, and read Robert Service's poems in the dugout Christmas Day. This letter seems to be catching up all arrears of information; but I must stop. How I wish you were here! The Home where Arthur is, is No. 8 Michelham Convalescent Home, Cap Martin, Menton. It is half way between Menton and Monte-Carlo.

The cold in England and France is appalling. From Havre to Paris the country was covered with snow, and in Paris the cold was intense. Women are on the trains everywhere, just as they are in England, "only more so." There was a grimness, too, that is wanting in London. All ranks and conditions are holding their breath for the great British advance. I think, if you come over, that we can persuade Arthur to come back. The London offer was from Sir Sam, and we must <u>never</u> forget it. I will talk the whole position over with Arthur and see what can be done. He will never return to the bank.

For heaven's sake do take good care of yourself, for I simply could not endure another strain.

Your loving mother,

Anna Durie

ARTHUR

My mother loved the south of France. Revelled in it. She visited the Monte Carlo casino and watched the proceedings, her heart aflutter at her own audacity. She spent much time at the Menton botanic gardens where crowned heads and heirs-in-waiting strolled before the war. She took an excursion through the old fishing villages; even went as far as Nice where from ten a.m. until noon the promenade is populated by the very cream of society. Mother adored that. Like the abundant flowers and the citrus trees, she thrived in the climate. She became a tourist, eager to cram her days with doing, thus allowing me to rest. Constantly to rest. She'd travel the town and its environs, take a drive to Cap Martin or climb the streets to the church of St. Michel, then make her daily report sitting to my left in the hospital grounds, eyes studiously avoiding the whipping right limb. I didn't mind. In fact I found it rather calming. The sessions with a doctor who minutely examined my history, my fears, my rationale for return left me with no wish to repeat such things to my mother. I wanted only the safe, the familiar, the comfort of her. I needed her, just as Thorn had, with a depth of longing I would never have imagined. I needed comfort and familiarity in the midst of confusion and dread.

———

I believe her frantic joy was fuelled by fear of my eternally vibrating body. We never really spoke of it. She simply said the shaking would cease as soon as the bronchial cough abated, that I was merely tired. And when the shaking ceased I could go home to Canada, or at least to an administrative job in London.

Mrs. Anna Durie has certain roles to play in life and rises to each of them perfectly: mother, widow, patriot, president of the Canadian Society for the Prevention of Cruelty to Animals, honorary lifetime member of the Red Cross, almost aristocrat, defender of society's mores. She lives her days cloaked in an invincible sense of her own rightness. Unfortunately, Menton's particular role was not one she could embrace – parent of a "shirker," an "incompetent," a "failure." She therefore existed in confusion. To accept her part, and mine, would mean a sea change in her ordering of the world. Months earlier she'd given an opinion of neurasthenia: a disease caused by weakness in the family line or a deficiency in upbringing. How could my violent tremors be explained when she believed such sufferings were cowardice? So many soldiers receive terrible wounds yet come through mentally intact. My lung injury had proved an aristocratic strength of will and innate bravery. And other men of lesser gifts survived the horrors with minds as fine as ever. So, therefore, if a man actually broke, it was because of a fault within his very makeup, a blemish previously unrecognized. Now she was required to process a Durie breakdown. File it within her passionate and very definite beliefs of who and what we are.

It was too much. Instead my mother chose ignorance of me and of my fellows. She did not give other inmates at the home the attention she bestowed on the patients at Étaples or London or Brighton. She never inquired if any of them was a duke or an Honourable, never wanted to know the availability of sisters or the location of country estates. She was amiable enough, smiling pleasantly at each as they stuttered and juddered their way along the corridors, giving a brief hello on the seafront or momentarily tearing her eyes from the vista to nod good day. But that was the limit of her intercourse. She wanted neither friendship nor commerce. She wanted no hint of cause and I had no wish to enlighten her. I wanted her chatter about the casino, the mule ride, tea with Madame de Billets. I wanted gentle trivia. Anyway, could anyone, even those starched collars toiling at the Royal Bank, imagine not simply what Arthur

Durie has seen but what he has done? The deceivers, the fucking liars who write the newspaper stories, insist we are noble,
brave gentlemen whose code is fair play; family members
assume we uphold the values of king and country, doing our
bit to ensure the continuance of civilization. No one wants to
hear another side. And we don't want to tell. We don't want
to see how close to the surface is our savagery.

I met up with Dick Joyce a few months ago when we were
both on leave in London. He used to be a lieutenant in the
58th, a machine gun officer who signed on just after me and
lasted until June 1916, when he was transferred out to something a little more mundane. He'd been a sales manager in a
paper company in civilian life; an ordinary man with a shock
of brilliant red hair. The men used to tell him to pull his hat
down hard else the Boche snipers would think someone had
struck a Lucifer and shoot the flame. A strong, solid, sensible
man. An honourable man.

While I'd lain in clean hospital sheets in Étaples, he'd faced
that third German attempt to snatch back the Ypres Salient.
The artillery attack went on for days. Gerry Cosbie was
wounded, and so was Cusler, his leg shredded by shrapnel.
A lot of other men were lost in what was fierce, filthy fighting. Joyce still looked done in when I saw him months and
months later. Neither London nightlife nor Westminster even-
song can make us forget.

We sat in a pub on the Thames at Chiswick, one of those
where people have had a mug of ale for centuries. Smugglers
used to slip in along that very Strand, matching their dealings

to the tides. I'm not sure why I feel the need to quiz each landlord, deacon, and concierge as to the history of a place. I feel a building through the flesh that once experienced it, not the statutes and bylaws that controlled it. Some essence of who we are seeps into the bricks we inhabit. Suffering haunts the soil and evil deeds committed within that locale take form. Such evil can consume a soul. No matter how idyllic a man's childhood or how many times he recites the Nicene Creed, he can be wrapped in its quilting as surely as if it were his shroud. It consumed Dick Joyce in Sanctuary Wood.

Watching the river run that autumn evening, Joyce exuded hatred. It oozed from his pores. He stared across the water and softly itemized the features of German "swine": square heads, pig eyes, face and development of the criminal. I'd heard it all before from others. Out on the river, Oliver's Island looked back at him. Cromwell reportedly camped there, plotting yet more murder and retribution.

Interesting, for a man to believe we are all either saint or sinner. To know beyond a doubt he is chosen, he is of the saved, that whatever his decisions, they are all correct, blessed by God. But at times, dark terrible times, Cromwell despaired. And he knew just as certainly that he was a sinner and God had turned His face away. That no matter how much he tried to live a good life, his future held only the irrevocable flames of damnation.

I'm not sure Joyce was talking to *me* that evening. Just to a soldier, a bank clerk who like him had evolved into another soul. One who wouldn't judge.

The Hun bombardment had decimated the Salient's three flanks. Heavy guns and mortar blew the Canadian front line to pieces and the German infantry rolled in to take over. But our support lines held and the corps regrouped to counterattack. Joyce and his company moved through Sanctuary Wood, "an oddly beautiful name for one of the suburbs of hell."

"I was in charge of A Company," he told me, "or those that remained. We entered the Maple Copse dressing station. I remember the silence. Everyone in there was dead. They had all been bayonetted. Perhaps the Germans were short of ammunition. Some of the wounded were lying straight and calm, unconscious when death came through the door. Others were half on, half off the bunks, deep defence wounds on their hands and arms. One man had fought like the devil. The bones of his fingers were visible where the bayonets had ripped, and his calves were hacked in a dozen places as if he'd kicked and booted at his assailants. A long clean tear ran from his rib cage to his groin, then veered sharply to the right. His innards spilled to the floor like sausage links.

"Pinky Campbell lost his footing in the blood and grabbed at the knees of the nearest man as he went down. But the nearest man was one of the dead. As the body slid from its place over the stretchered, it twisted and I saw the red dog collar. Stupid – but my brain plodded through denominations searching for colours. I knew already. He was a padre with a gaping hole across his throat. The blood soaking the starched cotton.

"An hour later we saw a group of Germans in the wood. About fifty of them. They held their hands in the air, lost, disoriented. They walked forward, giving us awkward smiles, eager to surrender. I watched as they moved toward me. I took silent pleasure in their naïveté.

"As the first dozen or so fell under the machine gun, I saw the startled looks on the faces of the rest. Those at the far end of the line had time to turn and begin to run. It was laughable. Some were still alive as I walked through the bodies. A saw-edged bayonet sent them to hell."

———

The Christian God wants us to turn the other cheek. The Jewish God wants vengeance. The Aztec God requires human sacrifice. Which deity to choose? I favour the multiples. The gods of the classical world suit my moods of late. There is no master plan, no benevolent Creator who loves us all no matter what our sins. Instead we are sport for the greater beings which choose to visit our world. I have seen the proof. Individual gods may intercede for us, some will even defy Olympus for the sake of mortal man. But they soon grow bored and we cannot rely on their concern. The flesh of soldiers who believe they have the answers, who see themselves as beloved, protected, chosen by a god who will fight the daemons wanting to wrest him from the earth, will drip from the mud as we repair our trenches.

I toyed briefly with conversion to Catholicism, my staunch Orange ancestors spinning wildly at the notion. Catholic clergy are in our battles, quite literally inside them. A safe, sanctimonious life is not their choosing. The Catholic dying require a sacrament of extreme unction, a final oiling. And it can't be done from the far end of a communication trench. Their priests are as much in shit and pus and blood as any soldier. I like that. I've heard too many sermons from clergymen who exhort us to take God's glory into battle yet wouldn't put themselves within a literal mile of artillery fire. Catholic priests expect much from their flock and give more in return. They will wipe clean a soul as long as the man promises to try harder. To start over. I would go far with such an abundance of beginnings. But my popish leanings did not last. I admired the priests, not their God who sent His only begotten Son to earth. In torment Jesus begged, "Let this cup pass from me." His father refused. He insisted on a slow, humiliating, agonizing death for the good of the world. He insists on it still.

—————

I sat in the gardens at Menton, surrounded by the camellias, close enough to the blue Mediterranean to hear it lapping the shore. Yet in the midst of such beauty I wanted only to get back to that place without a God. My mother insisted a Staff position was an honourable future. It didn't matter. Her purpose was only to give me comfort. She had lost her power to persuade.

I told her how the previous Christmas, the men of the 58th received an extra fifty francs to buy presents. Everyone marched from Battalion Reserves, where they were in rest, to Aubigny, shopped, and marched home in perfect order. But some of the money bought liquor instead of gifts, and an uproar soon tumbled out of one of the huts. Six men were drunk: singing, farting, and performing intricate balancing acts on the steps of the barracks as their companions cheered them on. A Staff officer pushed through the crowd and stared along the knife crease of his nose as raindrops ran along his red hat band. He declared the men a disgrace to the uniform. At the very moment his lecture began, the culprits, or most of them, attained that stage of drunkenness where bravado and honesty meet.

"You putrescent piece of shit."

There was a roar from the crowd.

A different voice: "What were you doing last week besides polishing your dick?"

"We were fighting our way up a German trench being shelled and machine-gunned. And you say we're a disgrace!" screamed another. "You jumped-up little arse-wipe with your polished boots and yellow streak."

The surrounding soldiers yelled encouragement, contributing their own adjectives, as their drunken comrades painted a detailed picture of the officer's minute prick, brains, and balls and his vast endowment of cowardice. His pinched face was crimson, as much at the shame as at the insubordination. They would be severely punished. No matter how safe, I did not want his life.

I looked up from my storytelling. Mother's mouth was set in a hard line. My language, she said, was disgusting. There was no answer to her comment. She left me and walked to the old town, to the church of St. Michel, to pray for my deliverance.

ANNA

I saw no shame in my pregnancy – William and I were already betrothed. It is only the middle classes who fail to understand; nobility has always recognized a betrothal as tantamount to marriage. But my father refused to acknowledge such things. His wild temper exploded and I had to steel myself to remember that union with the Durie family meant I had moved beyond my father's world. He raged through the house, his face twisted into the ugliness of his Hibernicized ancestors. And all his gracious manners and fine clothes abandoned him. He bellowed twenty different ways in which he would kill the "banjaxed decrepit gobshite." My sister, Emily, cowered into the folds of her gown. His words spat into my face.

"I *will* kill him, Anna. How dare that cute hoor bring shame to my house. I will not attend the wedding. I will not pay for the wedding. And if I do ever look on that man again it will be when I kick the dirt into his grave."

"Then I will cut the head from his corpse, Papa, and bury it in a pot of basil and die from want of him."

Papa stared at me.

"I am already his wife in the eyes of fifty generations."

He retreated, but remained true to his word. Only William's death brought him back. He attended the funeral and could not help but smirk when he threw a handful of soil upon my husband's coffin.

———

We married in the Catskills, and Arthur was born there six months later, more than fourteen hundred miles from my childhood home. Emily accompanied me, but Papa had forbidden her to sign any legal document, so William's friends, our hosts, acted as witnesses to the wedding.

And when my husband died, only five years later, I knew that if I began to cry I would never stop. So I did as he would wish. I remained faithful to his memory. I raised up his son and daughter to understand their heritage, their position in life, that to which their birth entitled them. I raised Arthur to be his father's son.

ARTHUR

The Menton doctor listened to my tales of routine and blood and death; of my parents, my job as a bank clerk, my terrors. It was as if he weren't truly there, just me telling my tales to the air. Sometimes he wanted me to talk of the good things in life. The memories I treasured. I told a story of love, of Eva, as if she resided within the pages of Ovid or the Arabian Nights. My life, but not my life. A novella set within a fairy-tale castle starring a man I might have been, a man I could become. And I saw there was nothing I wanted in Toronto, no reason to return. No real love waiting for me. There is a stolid little house I loathe and a mortgage I cannot afford. There are questions of whether it's possible to buy a motor car, of the right clothes, the right tableware, of whom I should dance or socialize with, and of promotion – when? what? how far? I need fewer questions, less mattering. I need more joy, just the occasional glimmer. And as I talked I slowly realized that George Thorn and every other man had the same war as I: hideous days punctuated by glimmers of light – a good meal, friendship, brief moments of tenderness. I understood. I had given to Thorn the last of his glimmering moments. My hand across his forehead was comfort, the knowledge that someone within that futile world cared, that he wouldn't die alone.

One night at Menton, as Thorn lay next to me and his artery sprayed its contents onto my pyjamas, I didn't try to speak. I simply listened as he said thank you, and I stroked his brow with a steady hand. He still visits me now and then. Still saturates me with his blood. Again I stroke his brow.

How can Dick Joyce explain to others? How can I?

❧

France, 19-3-17

My dearest Mother,

Will you send me two boxes of Allenbury's Eucalyptus and Menthol cough drops. If you can't get Allenbury's French Eucalyptus and Menthol cough drops will do. Send me also two boxes of bromo-quinine tablets. I am feeling fairly well; no cough or cold; but I want to have plenty of medicine. Please send it as soon as you can. I am still in billets and have not seen Colonel Genet yet. I have not received any letters from you, except three that came together, which I acknowledged.

With all the love I have
Your affectionate son,

Arthur

ARTHUR

German heavy artillery crashes above me, shakes the mortar from the walls. This cellar runs forty feet into the earth, the building over it long crumpled into brick dust. It smells of piss and damp, and the rats think it's wonderful. They no longer even scamper when the bombs fall. They swagger through the rooms like proud owners of a château, lazily investigating every pocket, satchel, and sock.

Down here I fill in forms, study battle plans, listen to pleas and whines. I count my lice, my soldiers, my aniseed balls. I write letters of condolence and recommendations for honours. And I supposedly censor the mail of those in my platoon; such an invasion of another man's life. But it is only pretend. They sleep on the fire step, shit in a mud hole, queue to fuck a whore in a brothel. Their purpose is to be shelled and shot. I can at least give them this privacy.

I wonder what my father would have done. Would he have followed the order to take away a man's dignity? It's impossible to know with any certainty. He gathered eight separate militia companies and, despite egos and rivalry and pettiness, forged them into one whole, the Queen's Own Rifles. He saw himself as a protector, fighting and petitioning for anything that would make them stronger, better organized, more effective. When the government forced him into retirement with two years' pay and no pension he was bitterly hurt but never lost his love for the men. Would I have been a different man if I'd had the opportunity to talk to him as I grew up, to learn from him? Would he have accepted the man I grew to be? Or would I have been as invisible to him as I am to my mother?

He died when I was four but I carried him with me. I used to talk to his spirit. My favourite place was the pond behind the big house on Spadina Road, where his dead self sat on the bank and watched as I sailed my toy boat – a miniature replica of his old schooner. By then the pond was a sad overgrown thing, a tangle of reeds and scum with no gardener to care for it – a wondrous place for a boy. I'd trap the water boatmen and the beetles and have them act as pilots as I told my father my troubles. I wanted him to be proud of me. I needed his help. I needed him to rescue me.

"Poor . . . low . . . out of his depth," the masters wrote on my school reports. I was "slow" at geometry, "weak" in Latin, "trying my best" in arithmetic. Learning came so easily to Helen; she teased me unmercifully. For me it was agony. When I left Upper Canada College, old Parkie, the head, described me as a "thoroughly straightforward and gentlemanly fellow, respectful, obedient, painstaking, and persevering." All very commendable, but not a word about my academic achievements. The things really important to schoolmasters escaped me. Yet I could control a stallion, and wild things would eat from my hand. I could name the birds and discover their nests; I knew the salamanders who came to visit, and watched the life cycle of the dragonflies. I'd wade through the muddied water, searching for frogspawn, and tell my father of my days.

He'd nod at appropriate moments. Sometimes he'd purse his lips then blow the schooner across the pond, sending the pilot scurrying over the side. And when the sun began to sink and I could hear voices calling from the house, I would sit astride his knees and draw my fingers through his whiskers and ask him to appear to Mother, to speak to her. He never did. Or perhaps she never listened. She had her own concerns. Each day the mail brought demands for money. City taxes went unpaid, the mortgage was attended to sporadically, servants left at dead of night taking silverware or bedding or the contents of the pantry in lieu of wages. Mother slowly closed up rooms until we lived in a concentrated cluster in the centre of the house. Kitchen, living room, bedrooms were all stacked above one another to draw in the heat, and instructions were to never let outsiders wander the hallways. Always the facade of comfortable gentility. I missed two terms at UCC because of illness, though I suspect Mother lengthened my convalescence because of our penury. Months of lying in my room drinking sweet tea and glycerine; of walking a prescribed distance each day; of riding when family friends allowed me the use of their horses. I carried a rash on my face, a rough, angry thing that crept over my cheeks and into my hair, flaring into painful blisters. Even when it faded, leaving only a dry flaky residue, Mother kept me home. Borrowing books from the school in order to continue my education, teaching me herself.

The last time I saw my father's spirit was the day we moved to a row house on Avenue Road. He had built Craigluscar for my mother when they were engaged. It was his dream, and hers. He waved a gentle goodbye.

France, April 18th, 1917.
After the Battle

My dearest Mother,
I have just received ten of your letters and have opened the last four. I am so sorry to hear that you were worried.

I have been all through the battle, and was on the ridge, though at the beginning we were in reserve. It has been a long tour; but I have been in the battle since Easter Monday. I was lent to B Company, and during the fight I had one of their platoons; now I am back with A Company.

It was terrible. We advanced to take over from the attacking Battalions and came in for very heavy shelling while we were relieving. Two or three times I thought it was all up with me; but God was watching over me. Quite often, during the very heavy shelling, I called on Him to help me.

We followed up afterwards and again, for about three days came in for very heavy shelling, but I did not get even a scratch. I shall not describe the scenes on the ridge after we advanced. We are in billets now, and I do not know whether we are going into rest for a while or up again for a short tour. Personally I think it is a rest for the Divisions. We will hope so anyway. If we go up again for a short tour I shall be as careful as possible. I have been to hell and back again.

The Germans are not such wonders after all. After the British bombardment I saw some of them behaving like children, I mean the prisoners coming through our lines. I have been living in their dugouts and they are well fitted with comforts which they had to leave behind in their hurried retreat. They are beaten and they know it; but it will take time to get them.

With all the love I have, dearest Mother,
Your affectionate son,

Arthur

I have just received your package and the medicine: thank you very much indeed.

A

ARTHUR

Preparation for the attack on Vimy Ridge involved every Canadian soldier. Working parties streamed over the landscape, bridged our trenches for an easy pass, and cut through our wire to facilitate the advance. Out in no man's land we dug a narrow furrow three feet deep that would be a jumpoff when the final orders came. Three men from my platoon – men? two aged twenty-one and one just nineteen – worked at my side. There was little conversation, not least because of the noise of the constant bombardment. As we'd waited to move out they'd whispered of rice pudding: Private John Hinscliffe describing his grandfather's cooking. But now there was no more talk of diet or memory, just the agony of imagining rising cream seared to a thick brown skin ready to melt upon my tongue. Our purpose was simply to dig the furrow and leave as quickly as possible. Then a roar of sound, black smoke spewing into the night. Hinscliffe's blond head arcing gracefully above it. I was jammed backward into the earth, as if someone had shoved my chest in a fit of pique. The three men were in pieces, like a child's jigsaw puzzle. Large sections, ready to be reassembled. One decapitated, two minus various limbs. Searle's right forearm tattooed with a horseshoe and the words "Good Luck" lay across my chest.

I wrote the obligatory letters to a mother, a wife, a grandfather. "Cheerful character . . . great friend to his comrades . . . you must only be proud." Interchangeable sentiments, condolences for the sake of the living, not the dead.

Hinscliffe was nineteen. Did his grandfather, maker of the peerless rice pudding, thank Juno for her kindness in bestowing what she said was every man's greatest desire, a quick and peaceful death? I doubt it. A little while ago the brass sent around a questionnaire asking if in case of our demise we'd prefer to be buried in our own hometown or in the country in which we fell, next to the comrades with whom we fought. Is it so important? Does Hinscliffe care if his head is in the same location as his torso? There were 104 battalion casualties in April and 11 missing. We bury men with the requisite solemn service, engraved cross, downcast eyes. A little while later their bodies are blown across the cemetery, seeded into the soil in a thousand different bits. What does any of it matter? All I need is a coin in my shoe to pay the ferryman.

I thought I would die that day, and if so I would die with pride. Immediately before the battle Alex Macfarlane, acting commander, gave final instructions to all officers in the minuscule shelter of a small wood. We had moved away from the men, and the open ground between us was plowed with shells. The air screamed and shook.

Macfarlane signed his 58th papers on the same day I did. A green lieutenant, a fruit grower from a southern Ontario village too small to appear on the map. I remember him waiting before me in the medical line, next to be examined by Cosbie. "Deep breath. Cough. Say aah." He looked fleshy and bewildered. I had no time for sympathy; I was too immersed in my own fear of rejection, my own legion of insecurities. There was a scar on his right shoulder, caused by a run-in with a farm machine as a boy, he was telling the doctor. I tried to concentrate on its puckered shine and, in an attempt to calm myself, to prevent my face from flaming, imagined the blade that had caused its jagged run.

Macfarlane's now a major, at age twenty-eight fast on his way to lieutenant-colonel, with umpteen honours, medals, and bars. I think he surprised himself most of all. He never had a hunger for glory, or a belief in a chosen destiny. He simply saw this as a job to be done: quietly, efficiently, methodically. He'd never commanded anyone in his life: not led the farmhands, or supervised office staff, or even corralled a brood of children. Yet it came to him as easily as breathing, with a calmness that invoked total faith. He led from the front, never sending men to do things he hadn't already done himself. He neither asked for promotion nor boasted about his deeds. He reported only the barest details of a successful mission: coordinates of enemy positions, number of prisoners taken. It was his companions who filled in the particulars, the destruction of a machine gun nest or fearless hand-to-hand combat. He is following a road, doggedly plodding along it, presuming it will eventually take him back to southern Ontario. He does not ponder his gifts, at least not aloud. What he thinks of within the silence is unknown.

My laconic style suits him. Macfarlane chose me as tentmate, sure in the knowledge that his much-loved quiet would be little disturbed. Our quarters became a haven of bridge and magazines. Cusler was our most frequent visitor and Dr. Jack Affleck joined our bridge games as soon as he arrived at the 58th last summer. A long-limbed Baptist whose sad face still betrays the adolescent embarrassed by his height. He had such a gift for telling stories. Macfarlane allowed entry to our card games on the condition that he relate a single adventure. Our camp table collapsed one afternoon under the weight of our laughter as he told of visiting a young lady in Montreal, the daughter of a medical colleague. A few days before this meeting the army had ordered his head shaved to the bone. The drastic barbering had coincided with the lancing of a huge boil on his top lip. Affleck's description of the girl's face when she opened the door, followed by how a crumb of buttered scone hooked onto his scab and, undiscovered, swayed delicately all through tea, caused our hysteria.

He had a pretty fiancée at home but lost his virginity to a prostitute when on leave in Paris with Jukes and an officer of his old field ambulance unit. He'd found the experience "disappointing." Then on that same trip he discovered Miss Shea, a Canadian nursing sister stationed in the city. They spent an afternoon exploring the finer points of the missionary position. The following evening their theatre tickets remained unused as she introduced him to further variations and the precise meaning of certain Latin verbs.

Cusler barged through the tent flap one afternoon not too long ago, bringing cold air and stomping feet and a stream of profane comments on the latest battle plan. Macfarlane simply nodded hello, gestured toward the recently arrived mail – a box of petits fours iced in violent shades of blue and green – and returned to his reading. I was at the table, writing to Helen some twaddle about the weather and Fritzy. Cusler stopped his tirade and smiled at me, a little grin of acceptance for our state. He flopped full length onto my bunk and took up the two dog-eared issues of *All-Story Weekly* that had landed there from who knows where. For the next hour he remained immersed in "Thuvia, Maid of Mars" and the only sounds were of him systematically licking the icing from a half-dozen of our treats. before neatly depositing them back among the brown wrapping paper. A private came to fetch him. Cusler's boot had barely crossed the threshold of quiet before I heard him regaling the fellow with a deafening exposition as to the effects of senior officers on a man's intellect. I laughed aloud. Macfarlane smiled: "I think we're winning him over."

Giving the orders for our part in the battle of Vimy Ridge, Alex Macfarlane could have been addressing a political meeting or giving instructions for the apple harvest – firm, focused – instead of standing within a hurricane. When the last detail was dealt with, the earth heaving, he said, "Gentlemen, you will rejoin your platoons." We moved into the open.

London, June 11th, 1917

My dearest Helen,
Oh, how I wish you were here! I really cannot bring myself to believe that you will not be allowed to cross. Something will have to be done. I wrote to you that I would cable the Secretary of External Affairs, asking him to issue a passport to you. In my letter I said that your presence was "urgently needed here." The last time I was at the High Commissioner's office I decided that the Englishman who saw me was rather a fool. The H.C.'s Secretary remembered me perfectly from last year when I was trying to get over to France to reach Arthur. You don't know how weary I am!

Sometimes I wonder whether it would be possible for you to get a Lieutenant's pay over here, whether you could take a position, and get leave, without pay, until after Christmas. I feel so sorry that you are not with me.

You know that I will do everything I can to get you over, but your side has the power. I won't let myself think you are not coming. Of course, here it is the food question, but this morning's "Times" has Lord Devenport's refusal to introduce compulsory rationing and that is reassuring. The meatless day has been done away with; but I am afraid it is chiefly to get rid of the problem of feeding stock. I don't think there is half the danger they make out. If you come be sure to give my address to the White Star Line (or any other) and I will do the same here.

Our afternoon tea has been cut off, so I am providing myself with an outfit. In my last letter I asked you to bring a box of loaf sugar. I hope your move back into the house will be right. I am dreadfully sorry about the Brazilian stocks and I think we had better not tell Arthur for the present.

This morning I received such a nice, coherent letter from Arthur. He and his batman, (Isn't it like him to take the batman along, out of harm's way!) are at the Divisional School for two weeks. "You would not think there was a war on and we are treated very well." He is sure to have written to you, so there is no use in my sending the letter.

Major and Mrs Rose came in at 9:30 Friday evening, having come up together from Canterbury in the afternoon. She is a mere shadow of herself and I found myself wondering whether she will ever see Canada again. There is no use saying anything more. Her husband says she must go home, but it would be impossible for her to travel now. They were only staying three days in London, on her account, and were not able to have tea with me at the Carlton. Major Rose told me all about Arthur and the 58th. Arthur wrote: "Harry Rose woke me up this morning to say good bye." Arthur, he says, is looking very well and is quite his normal self again. The 58th is still near Vimy Ridge. The Divisions take turns at the front, and go back, behind the Ridge, to rest. Lille is the objective; but, of course, there is much in between. I said to Major Rose, "I suppose there will be another terrible battle," and he answered "There will be another battle and four or five of them." So that is what we have to look forward to. The only time he was a little bitter was when I said "They are tremendously proud of you in Canada," and he answered: "And they have need to be!" and added: "If they are proud of us, why don't they send the shirkers over and more men to help us?" You see, that is the real situation. He was so grave that I could hardly believe he was the same man I knew at Bramshott.

To-morrow I am going to an afternoon tea and concert at the Royal Automobile Club, and afterwards I will go back to thinking of Arthur and praying for him, for I don't think "things" are very far off.

Yesterday I had a very fortunate experience. I went to Morning Service at the Abbey. Coming out through the nave I saw a small group, or procession of khaki-clad officers, who in some way looked extraordinarily strange; familiar and not familiar. Everyone was looking at them. A lady coming up at the moment, their leader stopped just opposite me to speak to her. After the first bewilderment I instantly recognized them for what they really were: General Pershing and eight or ten members of his Staff. I must say they looked wonderfully nice. As straight as arrows, gentlemanly, tall and lean and very soldierly. They wore a service uniform, high at the throat, and it was difficult to tell their rank by their dress. The General, who is to command the American Expeditionary Force in France, had some device on the front of his cap and two stars on his shoulders. The British Staff officer who was with them, some great man, I am sure, looked gorgeous beside them. They wore no leather strappings, but the peaks of their caps were brown leather instead of cloth. They went into Dean's Yard for a few minutes with the British Staff officer, and I waited until they came back and the autos drove off. Before they got into the motor in which three officers were already seated there was a moment's hesitation on the part of the British officer and General Pershing said: "Yes; this will be all right," and both officers popped into the car. I walked to Trafalgar Square through St. James Park at the back of the Horse Guards and into the Mall. The band of the Scots Guard was playing, something most unusual, there were crowds of people out, and the green of the trees was wonderful. I did wish with all my heart that you were there. I think the reason I enjoyed it all so much, was the knowledge that Arthur was out of danger.

I feel now as if we have gone the wrong way about getting you over. You should have gone to the member, and asked for some endorsement of you, which you could have given Ottawa.

I was very amused at "The Star" calling the 58th, "an all Toronto battalion." The two small things I sent you in the parcel, I bought at Roger and Gallet's shop in the Rue de la Paix, Paris. Tell me how you like "Mr. Britling."

Your loving mother,

Anna Durie

Anna Peel, 1879, when she was twenty-three and engaged to Lieutenant-Colonel William S. Durie.

Lieutenant-Colonel William S. Durie, First Commanding Officer of the Queen's Own Rifles, c. 1860.

Craigluscar in 1879, built by William Durie for his fiancée Anna. The original photo bears the hand-written notation, "Paradise."

Lieutenant W.A.P. Durie, 1915. The background around his head was blacked out when the photograph was cropped for his death notice.

Arthur Durie as a boy.

Arthur, Anna, and Helen on the steps of their St. George Street home in Toronto. Arthur bought the semi-detached house in 1912.

Helen Durie, 1914, two years after beginning her career as an English teacher at Jarvis Collegiate.

Anna Durie, c. 1915.

Officers of the 58th Battalion, 1915. Lieut. W.A.P. Durie is standing in the back row, third from left. Also shown are: Capt. G.O. McNair (third row, second from left); Capt. H.G. Cosbie, Medical Officer (seated in second row, second from left); and Col. H.A. Genet (second row, sixth from left).

Arthur seated between two unidentified Canadian officers, June 1917, at an Army Horse Show near Lens – just five days before he marched on top of the parapet during a heavy bombardment.

Lieutenant Elmo Cusler at training camp in England, early 1916.

Dr. Jack Affleck on leave in the south of France, 1917.

"Juksie" – Maj. Arnie Jukes, Buckingham Palace, March 1919.

Arthur's postcard of Wemyss Castle, Fife, Scotland. "My room" (where he slept) marked by an "X."

The beautiful Eliane "Ginger" Cossey.

Anna Durie in mourning, 1918.

Anna at Corkscrew Cemetery, Lens.
This photograph was probably taken in
August 1919, the first time she visited
Arthur's grave.

Grave of Captain William Arthur Peel
Durie, St. James' Cemetery, Toronto.
The cross of sacrifice was erected in
May, 1928. The original flat stone, 1925,
lies to the right. The inscription gives
Arthur's birthdate as April instead of
August: Anna maintained her fiction to
the end.

Loos British cemetery as it is today. The empty space in the foreground once held
Durie's grave. The cemetery holds 884 identified bodies and approximately 2,000
unidentified.

HELEN

The authorities will not allow me to return to England. The British government feels it already has too many Canadian women in residence, and with food shortages, U-boats in the Atlantic, a grumbling populace – well it is all too much for one nation to bear. So, with Mary now gone to do war work, I must stay in this house alone. I cook for myself, I clean for myself, wasted labour in these empty rooms. Arthur's salary is used to keep Mother in London, to support her vigil, while I remain in Toronto trying to pay a mortgage that is not mine. Mother never asks about the finances, Arthur is her primary concern. She writes of the Roman ruins at Ventimiglia, the flow of the Thames. She attends luncheons and concerts and is invited for gentle weekends in the country "to soothe her mind." To assuage her worries about her son.

In deference to circumstance, after I failed to rent the house, the bank agreed to temporarily reduce the mortgage payments. Acting for Arthur, I had to kowtow to a repulsive little man with skin the colour of overripe sugar plums, a pale yellow-green stretched across his numerous chins. He stared straight into my face while he quizzed me about Arthur's chances of promotion, Mother's hotel bills, and how much I spend on dresses.

"Considering you are thirty-four," he said, "do you think you may marry?" Yes, I will marry. And when I do you will beg for my business, and I will take it elsewhere.

Mother is angry with me, says I have not tried hard enough to travel to England or approached the right people. It is untrue. I have written to every level of government explaining why I should not be herded among the rest. I have tried to make my case. The truth is I desperately want to go. Anything to escape Jarvis Collegiate where the pupils are dull and the teachers duller, and Toronto where there is nothing except the embarrassment of my financial situation.

Mr. Cusler wrote twice in answer to my letters. Pleasant correspondence only. Then nothing more. Not that our friendship could be anything but casual discourse. My acquaintances are of a different caste to Mr. Cusler and he could only feel awkward in our company. But I think about the kiss. And about his words. "Let me inside you."

Toronto holds small men, insignificant beings of no consequence. Yet I have had my share of admirers. When I was at Columbia University, attractive, intelligent young men would seek my company. They were not what I desired, and I had time to wait.

I should be in Europe. It is unfair that Mother and Arthur are there. After the war I shall travel, while they stay in Toronto looking after the bills.

Perhaps Mr. Cusler will write again.

France, June 21st, 1917
Thursday, 9.30 A.M.

My dearest Mother,
We are now waiting to return. I am feeling much better and I have
no temperature. I am sending you a parcel to-day and will write

you particulars to-morrow. The M.O. here saw me this morning
and has permitted me to return, but I must report to our own M.O.
I shall get all my mail this afternoon at our transport lines where
we report, and will probably stay the night there.

With all the love I have.

Your loving son,

William

BILL

Divisional Training School. No subterfuge by Genet this time.
It was my turn on the roster. Two weeks of classroom with a
little light marching in the grounds of a fine château. Good
food, a comfortable bed. But the halcyon days were short-
lived. I suffered a recurrence of trench fever: 104-degree temperature, severe pain in my legs, an itch that near drove me
insane. I'd taken my batman along, he'd seen as much shit and
death as I had and was happy for the respite. But when I
became ill he didn't act as my nurse. I banned him from my
bedside. I'm not a good patient. I just want to be alone to
curse as long and as loudly as I wish. There was a small
infirmary at the château and once again there was much glee
at my propensity to swear in a variety of languages, dialects,
and funny voices. I'm glad I amused. When the doctor began
to explain my condition, how it is contracted only through
infected lice, I demanded, "Who the fuck cares?" So he left
me to my misery. It was not a bad attack as such things go but
my fever must still have remained when I wrote to Mother
and signed the letter "William."

I'd long ago accepted Bill from everyone, even the men referred to me among themselves as "our Bill." But I'd been careful to remain Arthur in my letters.

Mother had a conniption. I knew she would. She'd heard of it, of course. Officers on leave in London would chat and let slip "Bill," only to be firmly corrected. But that I should refer to myself in such a way, deny my own name!

Le Bel Inconnu finally discovered his identity. His skill and bravery enabled him to slay the scarlet giant, to ride tall through the haunted town, to stand fast as the shadows coalesced into an armoured fiend astride a horse breathing gobs of fire, to defeat that fiend and then remain silent and still as a glowing serpent wrapped around his body, flicking its slime-coated tongue against his lips. The yellow-eyed creature whispered his name. "You are Gingalin, son of Gawain, hidden and worthless until you proved your worth." And the coils slipped away until the long smooth limbs of a beautiful woman were entwined around him. His mettle had broken the spell which held her captive.

The Saturday I returned from training school was the second anniversary of the founding of the battalion. I remember how my legs were aching terribly, the residue of trench fever. There was a celebratory dinner in the evening and those who were able attended a horse show that afternoon. Competitions and displays and little booths where you could play ring toss or guess the number of buttons in a jar. There were buttery pastries and chocolate-drizzled sweets for sale. A skittles alley ran along one side of the tent and three different photographers set up shop under the canvas. Soldiers could sit on a folding bench next to a potted geranium and smile at the birdie. I was dragged by my companions to one of the seats and told to "be nice." The resulting photograph unnerves me. I sit straighter than the others as they crowd against my shoulders. I am pressed on but apart; a rabbit among wolves.

I'd found out that morning that Mother, despite all protest, was still worrying at the Staff in Divisional HQ, trying to manipulate a safe posting. As a result, I had been assigned a position in Ottawa at the Ministry of Militia and Defence. As if I would find a refuge in Canada. Another flurry of messages when I said no: give it to some Staff flunky who'd appreciate the largesse. Genet replied to HQ saying the army could not be seen to defer to the wishes of a soldier's mother, no matter how persistent she proved to be. They saw the logic in his argument and voided my orders.

I know that everything she does, she does for love of me. All to honour my name. She believes I've been deprived of my father's legacy. She is trying to restore my rightful place. I understand.

Once there were carriages and plumed horses driving up to Craigluscar, bringing officers and their ladies and the cream of society to the elegant Durie balls. I have no memory of this, though she tells me I was paraded in to be introduced and that I bore myself with great dignity. Mother has preserved the place cards from one occasion, made in the form of delicate fans that open up to show the colours of the Queen's Own Rifles. She wants such things for me. Society calling at my door to admire my dinnerware. Instead I choose to remain here.

I have done no brave deeds, garnered no great honours. I never will. But I have earned my name. I'm not the man who measured the fire step at Niagara with his swagger stick and declared it uneven. I have faced the monsters in the Forest Perilous and have not run from their terrors. My name is Bill, William as I now write it on my letters home. Arthur has gone away.

France, 25-7-17
5 p.m.
Second letter

My darling Mother,
This is just a very short letter. I have been sleeping pretty steadily and am feeling better. Will you send me a bottle of Anodyne Pine Expectorant and let me know about the insurance. Let me know too, when you leave London and where you go. I may wire you that I am in rest. If I do I will address the wire, "Mrs. Annie Durie"; but I think I had better not; the wire might frighten you. Do be careful about the air raids. I see by the paper of July 23rd that there has been another, but not on London.

My breathing has not been very good the last day or two, but a good rest will help considerably. We are supposed to drill and I hope to heavens we do not get too much, for I hate it.

There have been so many changes among the officers that I do not think my Blighty leave will be so far off after all; possibly October or November; so cheer up dear; it will not be so very long. I am very much afraid the war will go through the winter. I think about March 1918 will see the end. You can count on that, I think. Again, do let me know how you are and do be careful about the air raids. Where could you go? Would you go to Brighton? How I wish we were all together again as we were last summer; but cheer up! the main thing for me is to come safely through, and things look pretty good now, and will certainly quiet down in the Autumn; at least I hope so.

Write often to Helen; she must be broken-hearted at not getting over. Will you go and see Bob Pollock? I thought he was in Bristol; but from your list I am almost sure that he is in London. He is one of the officers in A Company. He will give you reliable news about me. He is an awfully nice chap. His name was on your list. I had just passed him when he was hit. Well, dearest Mother, I must end this letter. Do, if possible, see the officers, for you'll get all kinds of news about me; it is such a good chance. You might see Lieutenant W. H. Smith. He is also an officer in A company, and he had trench fever. He can give you reliable news.

Will all the love I have
Your loving son

       William

BILL

I will tell of the valour of Gilgamesh. How he knew the secret things, even those of the time before the Flood. How Shamash, the sun, gave him a perfect body. How Adad, the god of the storms, presented him with the strength of a savage bull and unlimited courage. So great were his gifts, Gilgamesh was both god and man.

"But, Mama, why must Gilgamesh battle the giant Humbaba? The monster has breath of fire, and jaws of death, and he can hear the wild cows move through the forest sixty leagues away."

"I will tell you these things, Arthur, but you must be patient. First you must hear how Gilgamesh and his friend Enkidu, his second self, went to his mother, the wise goddess Ninsun, and listened to her counsel."

Ninsun anointed her body with oils. She put on her most beautiful gown and glorious jewels to pray at the sun god's altar.

"Shamash, why did you give this restless heart to my son, Gilgamesh? He sets off to battle Humbaba. From now until the day he destroys the evil thing, do not forget him. Let your bride, Aga, the dawn, remind you of this. And each evening give him to the watchman of the night to keep him from harm." Then Ninsun called to Enkidu. "You are not from my body but you are as my adopted child. As the foundlings brought to the temple serve the temple you must serve Gilgamesh." She placed a golden amulet around the neck of the noble Enkidu, saying, "I entrust my son to you. Bring him safely home."

———

Lieutenant Arnie Jukes volunteers for every insanity out in no man's land. Despite the German bullets slapping into the earth around him, no matter how many grenades are lobbed in his direction, he survives. And he prospers from it. The man could fall in a barrel of shit and come up smelling of roses. He rarely speaks to me, recognizing I have nothing to give which could even vaguely help in his amassing of medals, bars, panegyrics, and promotions. His real name is Jucksch but it was just too German. When the newly minted Jukes laughs, which he does urgently and often, his left shoulder spasms and I am reminded of a Scottish terrier Helen once owned, before the milk horse kicked its yapping head into a passing Ford. Scratch one tiny point of skin below the hip joint and its ridiculous leg would cycle the air forever. The rhythm of Jukes's shoulder is its exact mirror. And his elfin stature is not much higher than the terrier's. He walks with a strange high-kneed gait like a prancing horse – perhaps caused by the lifts I know he fits into his boots. But put him on his belly and the man can move with the grace of a water moccasin. As he slides out of the sap and into the mud on one of his forays, his feet flick and his hips undulate across the morass until he fades into the darkness. He eats, sleeps, shits, and probably shags out there in an earth-covered hide no taller than the length of a man's forearm. He designed it himself – of course. He is proof of Darwinian evolution, proof that our amphibian ancestors crawled onto solid ground, feeling completely at home, but ever retained their desire to be wet and cold. Within a few hours he returns. As he rises from the putrescence of no man's land his buckle flashes along the one sliver of moonlight in the whole heaving mass, as if he dragged home a German batman to break out the Bluebell just outside the parapet. And there are spoils, always spoils. Sometimes a cache of arms. Once he stuffed a biscuit tin garlanded with cherry blossoms into the back of his trousers. It held a sweet bread kneaded into the shape of a swaddled infant, white with icing sugar. The raisins, lemon peel, and marzipan were washed down with the morning rum. The powder ghosted over our lips and into the grime of tunic fronts. Soon the flies abandoned their usual diet of putrefying flesh and entered the bacchanal of sugared serge.

Jukes's religion is unknown to me but I think of him as Puritan. Another Cromwell. Not for moralistic reasons, he visits the officer brothels as frequently as any, boasting of the moans he elicits from each of the whores, raising his voice to make sure everyone knows Marianne quite screamed at the size of his erect *bite*. No. A Puritan because of the conviction he is chosen. Even if he dies — slim chance considering his "speed, agility, and goddamn intelligence" — it will be as a favoured hero. A statue of George, the warrior saint, will rise above his grave. Instructions on dimensions and colour of stone have already been left with his mother. Extensive eulogies will appear in the quality newspapers and a phalanx of pretty girls, French, Belgian, British, and Canadian, plus German ones who've merely heard the rumours, will no doubt weep for the loss of the prodigious *bite*. I do not exaggerate.

Yet once I saw him in the Ypres ramparts, curled in one of the ancient casemates they use as offices. He was twisted under the legs of an easel, small as sixpence, almost invisible in the half-light. It was very quiet. No shelling, no sniper fire, no raucous water birds on the Ieperlee. Just his low sobbing creeping its way along the cold stone walls.

———————

Jukes was one of those sent to reconnoitre the German line just outside Lens, at Avion. The city fell in 1914 and we've been trying ever since to recapture it. It's where I am right now, yet again within the warren of workmen's cottages, or at least the rubble that remains, from where a single machine gun, hidden behind the brickwork, can destroy a company of men. His patrol made its way forward in a hail of grenades and bombs and reached its objective only to find it firmly held. When he made his report, the clean fat men far behind the lines ordered us to "capture and consolidate" Jukes's Avion trench. He'd talked of it as "strongly defended," of masses of equipment, of knots of enemy soldiers appearing from nowhere. Our job was to take possession, advancing "under a rolling barrage" in which our own artillery fires a line of shells directly over our heads. We follow in its slipstream, like the shooting party trailing the beaters.

I don't have the vocabulary to explain the experience of living within the barrage. There is not an iota of my previous life to which it can be compared. The words *noise, racket, din, cacophony* have no place there. The barrage is not a sound, it is a palpable thing. I am inside it and its exterior is another place. It presses against my skin and if I reach out my palm I can feel its waves. And if I push hard I am able to create a small hole in its presence, like the split second of emptiness created when I used to drive my hand rapidly through the bathwater. Then the water rushed back. I was powerless to dam even the narrow tub. The hole I create in the barrage is the gods' way of teasing me. At first I thought it was a tear that could only grow larger. My left arm and then my torso would discover the outside, the calm exterior. No. I was merely being shown what I could not have. I was reminded of the first brief successful days of class at Upper Canada College before more and more days crowded out what I had learned. And the clamour enveloped me.

At 2:30 a.m. the barrage began and signalled our plans to the Hun – so they'd know it was time to fire their machine guns. I flattened myself into the soil as did every other man in the platoon. Germans trying to kill us from one side and our own artillery making a similar attempt from the other. Then the barrage jumped forward and, inexplicably, the machine guns stopped and we advanced up the slope toward the remnants of the village. Pacing out my steps, trying to maintain a rhythm so I didn't crash into the wall of explosions; stumbling through fresh shell holes, swaying as the ground heaved. Suddenly the barrage lifted, and the silence poured in. To the right, gunfire and shouting began from where B Company was attacking Amble trench. To the left, our second platoon came under fire. Avion trench produced no sounds at all. I knew they were waiting for us. Bayonets fixed. Potato mashers and pineapples piled ready to obliterate a man's face or spill his intestines to the earth. I'm not afraid to die. But I am afraid that death will come slowly. I am afraid of weeping, of emptying my bowels, of lying in the darkness feeling the rats feed on my wound. I was afraid that the first man who tumbled out of that German trench would be resolved to kill a whole slew of Canadians, and would therefore be shoddy in his work. Or perhaps be vindictive, merely slicing one tendon and a bit of kidney, leaving me to bleed into the mouths of vermin. Still no movement from the enemy. I led my platoon to the left, through the noiseless twisting corridors. Nothing. We threw grenades into the dugouts: deep cellars tunnelled one into another through the long straight streets. No one emerged, bleeding and sputtering and desperate to surrender. And when we crept through the dark holes, no bodies were crowded into the corners searching for shelter. Empty. Evacuated.

Men carry talismans: a cigarette case that stopped a bullet, a pressed flower from the banks of the Humber, a handkerchief imprinted with a rouged kiss. They hum certain songs, follow a particular ritual. Such superstitions litter the line, rotting along with their owners. No need for talismans or rites. I felt the realization thud into my chest, permeate through to my fingernails, the ends of my hair. I *was* chosen. And my choosing was greater than that of Jukes. There would be no death. The gods had decided.

This wasn't necessarily good. It suggested some important destiny I didn't want. But I did want to live and screamed my yes into the air.

I thought Eos flashed her compliance across the sky. No. It was Fritz shelling the trench. That's why he'd left so fast. He knew this place perfectly and lined his guns to destroy it. But I wouldn't, couldn't die. I clambered onto the parapet as the air shattered with light and sound. I marched. I sang my triumph.

"The bells of hell go ting-a-ling-a-ling, for you but not for me."

Turn.

"And the little devils have a sing-a-ling-a-ling, for you but not for me."

Turn.

Voices from the funk holes shouted for me to get down.

"O death where is thy sting-a-ling-a-ling, O grave thy victory?"

It was Cusler's long arm that reached up and pinioned my calves. Then he yanked me forward, his free hand splaying against my chest to prevent my body from crashing on top of him.

"What the fuck are you doing?"

"Marching," I replied.

His face twisted with anger and hands the size of mud flaps dug into my tunic, lifting me four inches nearer his own height. He hissed into my face: "I refuse to tell your fucking mother you are dead. Do you hear me?"

"I'm a soldier. I march. It's what we do. And I will not die. I am a chosen one."

I thought he was about to slap me. Men were staring out at us from the scrapings in the trench walls, grateful for any diversion from the tedium of being shelled. I prayed it would be a punch, not a smack as if I were a child. But his anger pushed me away so rapidly I spun in the air and thudded into the wooden slats lining the trench wall. The metallic taste of blood flooded my mouth. I forced it through my teeth to drip down onto my sleeve. Another wound stripe. Then I was stumbling after him, his fingers threaded into my belt, until the crenellations of the trench offered an unoccupied corner, safe from curious eyes. His mouth was at my ear, that one hand again hard at my chest.

"You are insane. Take the job in Ottawa."

And now his hand was as nothing compared with the pressure in my breast. And I was the one enraged. He was too close for me to get any real force into my arm, but I clenched my fist and smashed up into the curve of his jaw. His head snapped back and he yelled something unintelligible. He must have bitten into his tongue because the blood ran from his mouth and I was elated. Another blow to the jaw while the surprise still held him, but the angle was wrong and my knuckles merely scraped over his cheekbones and jammed hard against his eyebrow. There would have been a third but his boot whipped into my ankle and I was down in the dirt, Cusler's frame effortlessly immobilizing me. And I felt my madness end.

He says I am his still centre, that in my presence his fires are banked and he can rest, that I expect nothing from him. It isn't true. I crave his strength of character, his strength of purpose. I felt his body pressing into mine and wanted some of that strength to seep inside my skin.

His eye was almost closed, already swelling beneath the fall of dark hair, blood smeared across his chin. He looked like a street urchin. I wanted someone to call that it was time to come home for dinner and to make sure he washed his hands and face. Then he'd go away from here and be safe.

Instead his platoon was ordered to penetrate further into the ruined suburbs that evening and establish an advance post on one of the mining slag heaps. They did it with twenty-six men to attack three hundred Germans and managed to hold the post for three hours, surrounded on three sides. A report came back he was dead, then he was captured, then he actually returned, grinning like a wild man, with thirty-five prisoners, two machine guns, a hole in his helmet and a gouge out of his skull. He went down to HQ to be debriefed, waving as he left, as if he were off to do a little boating at Sunnyside. And I was made a captain.

London, September 15th 1917

My dearest Helen,
Arthur sent you a cable the day he arrived saying he was here on a ten day's leave. This is the first moment I have been able to write, though I purposely did not write the first two days. When he came into my room he made the impression on me of a broken old man, but my common sense told me he would get better after he had rested a little. And that has proved to be the case. This morning, for instance, although we spent a delightful but tiring afternoon at Brighton, he looks much stronger. After he goes I will write you a long letter about him. This morning I have to get a letter off to Mr. Ridout, and there is not one second.

I have been fortunate enough to meet Mr. Cusler twice, and he has given me a good deal of information. You know he has been simply heroic. He says they call Arthur the bravest man in the Battalion. "He is absolutely fearless," is what he actually said. Then he told me what Arthur had not told me: that he found him on the parapet at Avion marching up and down while the men were in the trenches. He says that in A Company they are all trying to get him away before another push, and he added "Major Macfarlane says it is sheer murder to send him into the front line." They realize that his health is hopelessly broken, and so does he,

and it is making him wild. He will write to you. Meanwhile I am
very anxious about you.

I don't think you can be writing to me because I never get a let-
ter. Your last came through very quickly and was dated August 16th.

Arthur and I went to Windsor and we have been several times
to the theatre. After he goes I will tell you everything.

Your loving mother,

Anna Durie

Soldiers are given a cable rate of two-pence-halfpenny a word.

BILL

She watches me sleep. Often when I was at home in Toronto,
I would awake to the click of the doorknob as she quietly left
my room. When questioned she explained she was checking
if I needed anything to eat, if I'd left the house, if I'd called
to her. I think she needed to know if I still existed, this man
she'd invented. I think she would study me as I slept, discover
a warrior's eyebrow, a hero's drool.

She does it still. On leave in London, I arrived at her
room in the hotel, kissed her cheek, and lay down on her bed.
Immediate, deep, restful sleep. Hours later she said she had
been content to write her letters and quietly watch me breathe.
There is a comfort in her presence that cannot be attributed
to the softness of the mattress or the lavender of the sheets.
Something that takes me to a place of greater safety. I can't stay
in such a honeyed sanctuary, but for a while it is good to rest.

Later we sat in the dining room overlooking the green-sward, dabbling with a much depleted tea table. There is voluntary rationing in effect in England: bread and sugar are in short supply, and hotels have instituted days without meat and potatoes. Food queues are common and prices high. Mother does not complain of these things, deprivation shows she is doing her part in the war effort; it is bureaucratic restrictions that cause her to lament: "No ordinary power will drive the Englishman out of his rut and from his red tape."

Now she has returned to Toronto to aid Helen in her troubles. I'm not sure exactly what those are. It seems Helen is unable to cope with matters. Mother says there is some conspiracy afoot at Helen's school, jealousy at its root. Its details escape me. Why anyone would be jealous of the Duries' genteel poverty is beyond me. But Mother insists it is so.

I recall the faint hum of street traffic wafting toward our sparse table. I listened to her gossip, the minute details she gives about the lives of her acquaintances. The banalities of existence continue, will always continue, no matter the wars and battles. I am glad of that.

Passschendaele

. . . .

I pray you for an instant follow me
In thought to Flanders; take at Ypres a train
And push towards the east; then make descent,
After a twenty minutes' run by rail,
Then take the road, and stand and laugh to scorn
The shell-holes on the Ridge, remembering well
That every pockmark meant a human life.
Look down; now throw your swimming eyes across
The path of glory stretching to the east.
For here it was the 58th was given
By luck, the honour in the attack
At Passchendaele, the fight, that brought us all
An everlasting fame, and made us great
And more than glorious at a staggering cost.
Now, thread your way between the humps and scars
And you will come, in time, to Bellevue Spur,
Rather, let's say, to the enchanted ground,
Where the old battalion, plunging up the slope,
Tho' met with withering fire from the Huns,
Swept on, till only seventy were left,
And held the Spur.

Anna Durie

BILL

King Gralon, ruler of the Bretons, sired a beautiful daughter whom he loved above all things. He built for his child, Ahes, a magical city of brilliant palaces and magnificent squares, of meandering steps and impossible steeples. As Ahes grew to womanhood, young men would travel across the lowlands and along their waterways to the fabled Ker-Ys, nestled safe behind its gigantic dikes, to glimpse the graceful maid. But a maid she was not. During the daylight hours she drew young men to her beauty and in the darkness drew them to her bed. Bewitched them. Amid the secrets of the night, they were blind to her evil ways and instead saw only the perfect curve of her breasts, the dark well of her eyes, and would discharge any commission to return to the bindings of her thighs. Her lovers became her dunnage, to do with as she willed. In the alleys of the city they would steal, maim, and murder at her command. And when she tired of each man's fawning love she would strangle him with her copper hair, push his body over the dike, and watch him float to sea. Only the old courtier, Guenole, suspected the vileness of Ahes. He tried to tell Gralon of his daughter's wickedness, but the king would not listen and young men continued to die.

One morning, as a golden boy spun upon the tide, a stranger entered the city. He was clothed in red armour and his eyes burned like flame. Throughout the day Ahes played the coquette, but control belonged to the red knight. He promised his favours only if she followed his commands. And his command was that she open the city's floodgates. Thinking only of her pleasure, Ahes used all her strength to turn the massive key. As the water began to rage through the streets, as the skies opened and the rain fell in torrents, the princess screamed for her red knight to come to her, but there was no reply. The dikes shattered under the onslaught of the waters. The citizens of Ker-Ys were swept into the tumult. Uncaring, tired of Ahes's evil ways, the gods simply watched. King Gralon saddled his strongest horse and lifted his daughter behind him, spurring the beast through the current. Guenole followed in his wake. But the sea boiled around them and their efforts were as nothing. Ker-Ys and its people disappeared beneath the swell.

"Only if you throw off your daughter and her murderous ways will we be saved," cried Guenole above the roar. Yet Gralon would not abandon Ahes, not until the stallion screamed in terror and he felt his daughter's fingers clawing into his flesh. Only then did he recognize her barbarity and hurl her into the waves. Immediately the rains ceased and the wind turned to a gentle breeze. Too late. The city was lost.

Snared within the drowned buildings of Ker-Ys, Ahes lives. And still, in vengeance, she draws young men to her beauty. She leads them away from the safety of the solid pathways, stealing their breath, trapping them forever in the buried streets.

––––––––––

We waded to our waists in yellow mud. Yellow, the colour of dysentery. Seeping into gun barrels, coating teeth and eyeballs. We wore sandbags while our trousers dried, ate rations painted with filth. We lived in dung, as we prepared for battle. The Imperial General Staff decreed our objective as Bellevue Spur, a ridge of land to the northeast of Ypres, overlooking what once was the village of Passchendaele, now only brick dust. The late summer rains hadn't ceased at the arrival of autumn. Preparatory bombardments churned up the ground and destroyed the vestiges of a drainage system perfected over centuries. We laid duckboards along the ground in order to work, strips of wood joined by crosspieces. Often they sank or simply floated away. At best the land moved as we passed over it, the boards swaying under our tread; the slime was a living thing waiting to devour us. Men who slipped from the pathways were trapped forever and drowned under the weight of their packs.

Other armies had been there before. Their dead remained just below the surface of the sucking mass. We'd come upon them — a gaping jaw, a bloated belly — as we built new tracks across the mire to drag our artillery forward.

Through the night a heavy mist mutated into rain, a soaking drizzle. At 5:40 a.m. the barrage began. Seven hundred yards deep, thousands and thousands of pounds of shells, advancing a hundred yards every eight minutes. It obliterated the networks of roadways. I wasn't part of the first wave as it followed the barrage. I wasn't there when the artillery gunners to the right slowed down, lost their rhythm, and the men of A Company, my company, walked into our own shellfire. Instead I waited within the din and tried to see a thousand yards past the smoke and the eruptions of slime to make sense of anything at all. I couldn't even fathom why we were there. I understood Vimy, hideous as it was. But this possessed no logic. They were loosing the guns into a landscape devoid of solid ground, and sending our men to follow after. They murdered us. Field Marshal Haig had driven past us as we marched to Dieval; ordered his driver to slow down as he shouted out his pride in British soldiers. He couldn't even be bothered to get our fucking nationality right.

―――――――

I waited for orders, for a runner to tell me where and when. But when evening came it was Alex Macfarlane who stood in front of me. He stared, as if he wanted me to make it better, to light the lamp and send the bogeyman back beneath the bed. He was once again acting commander. Genet had issued the orders, given the rallying speech, and departed that morning on leave. Macfarlane held a cloth to his face to staunch the blood from an angry gash. Large patches of dry and drying blood stained his uniform, back and front. Their origins numerous.

"We're shot to pieces, Bill."

Then a flow of words tumbled from his bloody mouth. I was to organize an evacuation of the wounded, at least the ones they had been able to gather into one of the captured pillboxes on the height of Bellevue Spur. Scores upon scores of them, pushed into each other, one man's mangled flesh abutting another's.

I could barely find footfall.

Jack Affleck was already there, our latest medical officer, working feverishly on a heap of mangled flesh that screamed beneath his hands. He gestured to one, two, three who should go in the first batch, then realized he was about to include everyone in the place.

"Sorry. It's been a bad day. Your choice, Bill."

How to choose? The ones screaming the loudest? The ones lying in stagnant water? The dismembered? The unconscious? I had sixty stretcher-bearers, six needed per wounded man, maybe more considering the terrain, to move through a thousand yards of porridge. The arithmetic was irrelevant. I simply started at the doorway. It was that or step on ten men in order to reach one.

The night was pitch and landmarks non-existent. Not a stump or hedge to guide the way. Just shell craters and slime and broken bodies beneath our feet. Ridges of moist ground, narrow lanes of mud, an attempt to skirt the deep hollows. I led the way, stumbling and slipping each twenty yards or so, then falling. Testing what seemed solid to discover it was only crust and that I was taking my party into liquid mud to their waists. Grabbing onto the dead as I lost my footing.

So many had dragged themselves into the earth's depressions in a search for shelter. As the new shell craters filled with water the wounded slowly drowned. I could hear their noises in the darkness. Men do not often die with brevity. Sobbing, moaning, gurgling, screaming. Voices all around. Boys who recently lounged in the sunlight of college reading rooms, farmers to whom lambing and the wave of a barley field marked the seasons of the year, musicians who spent their Sundays in the polished oak of a choir loft and dreamt of solos. They lay out there now, dying.

Those soldiers would be meeting with the messengers. A whole universe of them were abroad, drifting over the land, trailing their fingers across trembling skin. I could see their shapes out upon the killing ground. The fanged Keres fighting among themselves as to which would drag a man's soul from his wounded body and then feast upon his blood. Shriker and the soft plop, plop of his paws. The silent fetches who for one heady moment seem to be comrades coming to the rescue but are discovered to wear each man's own face. Satan on his black stallion ahead of the hounds and riders, bearing down on his quarry. And Bean Nighe washing the grave clothes of those about to die. I could hear her keening. She was out there too, naked, ugly beyond credence, one tooth, one eye, her pendulous breasts swaying as she scrubbed the blood away. If a man can sneak up to her as she washes at the stream and suck at her breast he will be granted one wish. I would do that; I would risk her retribution and suck her wrinkled tit to obtain my desire, to bring my company home.

"Look without seeing," Cusler had said. But to hear without listening? I couldn't. Behind me, a sergeant lay upon a stretcher, his face sliced clean away. The workings of his rasping breath open to the air. I wanted to shoot him, save him the agony of his remaining hours and instead search for one of those voices in the shell holes. I wanted to give the order. I wanted responsibility to do a better job than the cocksucker God who was supposedly watching over us. And after that, my next responsibility would be the death of Field Marshal Haig, murdering us for that useless corner of field. Then his lackeys, too scared to tell him to stop, too scared to drive a bayonet into his arrogant gut. If he appeared before me I could do it as surely as I could suck Bean Nighe's foul pap. But I was supposed to put myself in God's hands, according to the chaplains, offer up suffering to His glory, bow down at His mighty works. I screamed my dissent: high, long, loud. And all went quiet. Every voice from the morass momentarily ceased. Every man heard my cry and knew its meaning.

A stretcher-bearer's hand was on my shoulder. Morley Hamilton, age nineteen, a butter maker in his other life.

"We should get going, sir."

He squeezed into the muscle, hard, steady. How can a butter maker cope with this? A man who is able to form something so beautiful, who stamps his achievement with a cross-hatch of grain to mark it as his own. How can he live in this place?

"The wounded need to get to the aid post," he said. "We can all scream with you, sir. But I think we should walk at the same time."

I made five trips leading sixty bearers, with four captured Germans roped in to help, back and forth. Between us we cleared the pillbox. Seventy men brought out, seeping through the canvas of the stretchers. Hours upon hours. On our last journey to the aid post I saw her clear, shining in the darkness. The shroud clothes hanging limp in her hands. Wailing into the wind. I knew I must approach carefully. Must quietly creep and in one movement reach for her wrinkled flesh and suckle. She would be trapped, beholden to me, forced to point the way to my company, to those missing men. I crawled on my belly over the moving ground. Jack Affleck called my name, but I had things to do.

Only yards to go before I reached her, when I heard the creaking of old wheels, the laboured snorting of oxen. Under the sallow moon I could see blind Ankou, Cain himself, walking steadily toward me. He wore a wide-brimmed hat low on his brow, like those favoured by ancient Dutch merchants, and his head twisted slowly from side to side as he sniffed the air for prey. His long fingers twitched toward the corpses, directing his minions to the dead. Ten grey forms tossed his chosen ones onto the cart. Two more standing atop the heap, neatening the pile so that yet others could be added, all the crevices filled. As he drew level with me, he stopped. His sightless eyes turned in my direction and his thin nose lifted slightly, the nostrils flaring. He smiled.

"Captain Durie. Good evening to you." His voice no more than a breath.

"Good evening."

He waited a moment and the wraiths waited also. I could think of no more to say. His head bowed slightly.

"Until later, Captain."

And on he continued. The wheels creaking after him, the workers high on the cart stacking the cordwood.

Bean Nighe had not wavered from her task. Not even raised her head to watch the exchange. I moved steadily. Determined to complete my quest. Knowing this was something I could do, one thing of substance. A lunge and she was under my hands, ice-cold. She didn't move, didn't twist away, waited for her fate, knew she must obey the dictates of her own myth. But I could find nothing to suckle. Her breast was hard and smooth. No place to end my mission.

I'd captured a corpse, hanging on the wire, naked, his body glistening in the faint moonlight. The skin of his arms hung from the tips of his fingers and waved gently over a gaping crater. For a moment I thought his head was bent, but it was gone. Just the final vertebrae rising from his shoulders. A man nameless forever. Below him, in the hole, eyes wide, staring at this creature, was one-half of Private Bill Dodds. Neat, proper, tunic unbloodied. A forty-three-year-old labourer who quoted Walter Scott to me when I asked why he'd joined up. "One crowded hour of glorious life / Is worth an age without a name." And so he had his crowded hour.

I searched until dawn for my soldiers and found no one. Twenty-seven battalion men. Lost in the buried streets.

BILL

Anything is for sale in Poperinghe. The streets overflow with plenty. Only five miles from Ypres and yet another world. There are red-light brothels for the men, blue-light brothels for the officers, chocolates and embroidered love notes to send to the virgin girls at home; liquor, sweetmeats, and perfumes. There are tailors and cobblers and tobacconists and wine merchants and barbers and hatters and Turkish baths. And there are restaurants of every description: coffee houses and steak houses and small *estaminets* serving egg and chips to suit the English taste or high-class bistros offering the finest cuts of meat and the best champagne. And in a class by itself is Ginger's.

Monsieur and Madame Cossey opened a little café at the beginning of the war, a modest enterprise serving the simple needs of the fighting men. But Monsieur and Madame have three young daughters, each more beautiful than the last and each endowed with flaming red hair. Madame taught her daughters well. They know how to charm the customers. They are never blatant, never crude; it is more the promise of a possibility that makes soldiers return. Softness and warmth and a movement of the hips never seen on even the prettiest batman.

The most beautiful daughter is Ginger, the youngest, only twelve years of age when the war began; lithe and supple, with the reddest hair of all, and a clear understanding of business. The establishment turned "officers only." Rumours surfaced about the girls, how their favours are discreetly available to a select few. But I never met anyone who could prove such a liaison.

Ginger is the crackerjack. Her greatest gift is her ability to welcome each officer as if she has been waiting just for him. The lieutenants see innocence hiding feral passion. The colonels suck in their bellies and swear they see a desire for experience and finesse.

When Colonel Genet returned from leave after the worst of Passchendaele he declared a special feast to honour the bravery of his battalion. He decided on Ginger's as its venue. We officers dined on sardines, mock turtle soup, and roast chicken with stuffing and bacon; there were baby peas and potatoes whipped with butter and cream; we had raspberries smothered in a velvet custard and tiny shortbread cookies studded with hazelnuts to finish; we drank claret and brandy and smoked fat cigars. Then the bill arrived. Genet visibly blanched and everyone agreed to divide the cost by our number. But our commander said no, the invitation had been his, he would cover it. He spoke to Ginger, asking details on each item; he adopted his pre-war authoritative pose, the chief accountant discovering the books are falsified, and combined it with the senior officer in total bluster. She had an explanation for everything and helpfully pointed out the best spirits, the fine wines, the select aperitifs.

There was to be no relief, and Genet returned to the table a defeated man. Jukes whispered retribution. If the colonel had to pay the exorbitant bill then he should at least get value for money. A case of champagne from those stacked near the door would accompany us back to billets. Jukes offered himself as the perpetrator, tall Jack Affleck would be the visual block, Genet the distraction.

But Ginger refused to be distracted; she ignored Genet's further protests.

"Send your general. I will speak to him," she laughed, and her fingertips trailed briefly down the buttons of his tunic. If she'd dragged that pale little hand on a return path he would have abandoned his scheme and settled for a private wank in his quarters. But she moved away too fast, deserting his gentle lust for the shrill demands of a whey-faced captain at a nearby table. Genet turned, his face gloom-ridden.

"Bill should do it."

Fuck! It was Cusler. He was smiling at me, hatching the plan as I squirmed. I didn't want to be any part of this ridiculous larceny.

"She likes him. She likes the quiet ones," he continued, buoyed by my glare. "He can create the diversion."

There was a snort from Jukes and sniggers from further down the table.

Their derision didn't bother me. Women did respond – Cusler once told me it was because I looked in need of an education. I'd said there'd been an excellent teacher, thank you, and I wasn't searching for another.

"I know," he'd replied. "Scotland. It was obvious. You carried round the just-fucked look for weeks."

Genet paid the bill and I stood, as the giggles crept over the table.

"Eliane."

She turned, a little surprised at the use of her given name.

"Yes, Captain Durie?"

"I was wondering. . . ."

She waited, smiling, amused by my hesitation.

"Yes, Captain Durie?"

"I was wondering if you would care to . . ."

She moved a little closer, only a fraction but enough to signal her interest in what I was about to say. Behind her I could see Affleck standing square to the room, supposedly chatting to Cusler but having a hard job not dissolving into laughter every time he caught my eye.

"Did you have something to ask me, Captain Durie?"

Perhaps he thought I'd be overcome by schoolboy blushes. I'd prove I could play my part. I gently brushed a strand of red hair behind her ear; she dropped her lashes, then raised her eyes slowly to mine.

"I wonder if you might help me with some French translation, Eliane?"

"But Captain, your French is excellent. You have spoken to me quite fluently on a number of occasions. I remember perfectly." She raised herself on tiptoe and moved a fraction closer so her hips brushed mine. "Perhaps there is something else you wish to ask?"

I gave her my version of an enigmatic smile.

Cool fingers drew my head down.

"Come tomorrow," she whispered, the renegade strands dusting my cheek. "In the morning time. You may ask me anything then."

There are women everywhere. I don't mean the tarts and prostitutes who populate every street corner, or even the high-class whores at tea dances and socials. I mean the well-brought-up young ladies who ask after my family's health and suggest we might "become friends." Every mother wishes to introduce her daughter; every daughter wishes to escape her mother. The sight of an officer sends them into heat and, as officers are everywhere, their state is constant. A wound stripe on a tunic sleeve is particularly appealing.

"Are you in pain? . . . Is there a scar? . . . Would it be forward of me to ask to see?"

"Well, that would necessitate removing my tunic and shirt."

"I promise I will close my eyes, Captain."

Many officers choose instead the company of nurses. They understand something of our world; are practical, not star-struck; and if a man reads the signals wrongly his suggestions are simply declined with a straightforward no, instead of a bout of hysteria. Nothing can be suggested to an attractive nurse that she hasn't heard a hundred times before.

At the edge of the doctor's broad shoulders I could see khaki arms slide a crate from the pile. The door opened, just enough, and Affleck, with his invisible companion, drifted into the night.

But Cusler stood there still, eyes narrowed in the smoke of his cigarette, as whoops of laughter filtered into the room.

"I must see to my customers," Ginger said. "I hope you will visit me, Captain Durie." Those slim fingers removed an invisible fleck from my tunic and she was gone into the hubbub.

Outside, the champagne was nowhere in sight. We clambered onto the wagon, and as it turned the first corner Jukes appeared from the shadows, his face a mask of woe.

"I dropped it. Every bottle smashed."

Groans and curses, until we saw his grin.

"Would I let you down, boys?" and he swung the crate onto the wagon bed. A dozen hands grabbed at the bottles as he vaulted aboard, already editing the adventure.

"Did you notice how quiet I had to be? Of course, I had to steady myself for the weight, then . . ."

The corks began to pop.

Cusler thumped my shoulder. He stared at me across the top of a bottle, swigging its contents until his eyes widened and his stomach began to undulate, like a cat about to heave up a hairball. The champagne flowing down met the bubbles coming back and everything sprayed outward in an arc of froth. Gasping, gulping, snorting, laughing. My tunic caught most of the spume and he tried to clean it with his sleeve as snot and Veuve Clicquot dripped from his moustache.

"For God's sake, Ellie. You're making it worse. Move away."

But he didn't. He pulled me down to sit on the wagon bed and laid his head on my shoulder, taking desultory drinks or nursing the bottle between his thighs.

"Ever been drunk, Bill?"

"Never felt the need."

"Fucking Christ! We need it if anyone does."

We finished the champagne in the tent, plus a few more bottles. Macfarlane, Cusler, and me. Hushed, as ever; the canvas shrinking into the dimensions of our conversation: Genet's fatigue, Jukes's posturing, Ginger's breasts. Why I didn't explore them. Then other breasts, other flesh. The kind of women who loved us in return. Academics should have crowded at the doorway and studied our discourse. It was a treatise on longing. Half sentences of desire and its memories: taste, smell, contrast. Alcohol brought only sadness, and Macfarlane's rules on quiet were well suited to our yearnings. Cusler's eyes dampened as he reached completion.

Savoy Hotel
London
13th Sep 1917

My dear ones,
Still going strong just like Johnny Walker. The old legs are doing fine, should be fit for fighting again in a few days. Have been quite busy trying to get new kit and getting in claims for the kit lost as nothing I had on is quite fit for wear again.

I am very anxious to get back to the Bn but must wait for orders. War and the army certainly make the individual a small factor, but of course at times we can do quite big things. That is where the game comes in.

The cross is being sent on to you which should arrive in a few days. I enclose an M.C. ribbon as worn on the left breast on service dress. I am sorry I didn't get the DSO as well or a Bar to the M.C. for if I do say it myself it was a fine piece of work my last stunt. Such is war thank Heaven. I got promotion anyway so that helps a lot.

Quite happy to-day. I just got word that the young officer who was badly hit and who we all thought would die is doing fine. He is a wonderful chap. Just 23 and will stop at nothing. It hurt me beyond words to let him go over the top but they wouldn't let me so I stood and watched. He got hit. I saw him stagger and fall then jump up again and jump in a nest of Huns. His brain was then exposed and a wound in shoulder. He was the real stuff. I put him in for an M.C. I hope he gets it. I enclose his letter. I carried on where he left off and believe me we did slaughter those Fritz. I am so glad we did so well and that I was able to hang on until relief came. It was good sport and a joyous victory even if only a petty scrap. I enclose some white heather given me by Queen Alexandra.

Love and good cheer to all

Elmo

BILL

Elmo Cusler's body has been bloodied and battered three times, and still he returns to the lines. He says this is his calling and he lusts for the fight and its glory. In battle his eyes darken and he becomes something other. But there are times when all is too much, when the warrior is lost to the man.

Yesterday he disappeared inside himself and has not yet emerged. I've seen this once before. Then it lasted two days and afterwards he said the universe had shifted. He'd moved into a private place he wasn't supposed to be; there'd been some kind of cosmic mistake. So he made himself very still and waited for the mistake to be rectified. Macfarlane and Affleck understood. The doctor stared into his eyes, lifting the lids, tugging at the corners. He told me to look after him, that the simple act of being close was all it needed. Cusler would return when he knew it was time. Affleck is leaving soon, going back to his old field ambulance unit. I hope our new medical officer is as understanding. I hope he is more than morphia and bandages.

I know why Cusler disappeared this time. He killed a man, hand-to-hand combat, and it turned him inward. He was checking a captured trench and rounded one of the corners. There in front of him was a German private stripping the weapons from a corpse. A stack of rifles was cradled against the man's chest. Cusler had a pistol ready and a platoon close behind: he presumed the man would simply surrender. But instead the German heaved the rifle pile at Cusler so butts and bayonets clattered across his hand and the pistol tangled itself among them and fell to the ground. The man lunged and they rolled in the mud, feeling the steel blades slice their skin. The German was strong, and his legs twisted into Cusler's, pinning him sideways, one hand pushing his head into the earth, the other tightening around his throat. No leverage, no breath, and the belief that in one moment the hands would move slightly and snap his neck. Cusler's knuckles scraped against the rifle pile and he lifted and plunged, not knowing if blunt wood or sharpened steel would jam against the German's ribs. He felt the blade slide in without pause. The man said something but the words came out as only bubbles of blood popping across his lips. He seemed to talk forever. There was a cry from behind and someone dragged the weight away, Cusler's arm tingling with the shift of pressure.

He didn't tell me at first. He is a master at pretending, but to look at something and not see it is impossible when that something is dripping its red wetness onto your skin. I know these things. He has killed so many, but never so close.

It ate at him. All through Christmas I waited for him to explode. Now I'm glad he has disappeared into the stillness. I read aloud the poems of Robert Service that I carry with me – the dark ones; Cusler has no time for sentiment. And later, when he is well, we will debate their accuracy.

Chance! Oh, there is no chance! The scene is set.
Up with the curtain! Man, the marionette,
Resumes his part. The gods will work the wires.
They've got it all down fine, you bet, you bet!

It's all decreed – the mighty earthquake crash,
The countless constellations' wheel and flash;
The rise and fall of empires, war's red tide;
The composition of your dinner hash.

I will argue either side, revelling simply in the contest. I don't want him to know how the battalion is my safety. But perhaps he knows it for himself. How the sound of the guns, now crashing above me, once so terrifying, calms me, holds me in its palm.

France
28 12 17

My darling Mother
Just the usual letter, everything is about the same, though it is very cold and dry with snow on the ground. I am feeling pretty well and hope you will arrive safely at home. Give all the love I have to dearest Helen, will try to write every day to you, though it may be a little difficult, it is very quiet.
   With all the love I have
   Your loving son
                William

BILL

Acting Sergeant Major David Embree has arrived in the dugout, needing me, as officer in charge, to inspect Nabob trench, our front line, where the morning shelling has caused collapse. Embree took an officer's course at Dalhousie and hopes to attain the exalted status of lieutenant very soon. He is a good soldier though a little formal in his manner. I try to tell him not to be so serious but he remains unconvinced. If he reaches officer status he intends to make his career in the army after the war. I cannot fathom such an ambition, such a wish for permanent discipline. I will not return to the Royal Bank, that I know, but unfortunately the remainder is uncertain. I cannot see my direction. I loathed mathematics at school and I loathe it still. I refuse to spend my days in computation, whether or not it is a good profession for a gentleman. Enough of such matters. Cusler says we should be travelling minstrels, prowling through Europe in search of rich and horny widows. He is joking. There is a nursing sister he writes to constantly. She is different from the others. His face lights when he speaks of her and coordinating their leaves is his constant challenge. Maybe I will become a butter maker. I'd like to see the results of my work at the end of the day and feel pride in my creation.

Private Henry Gordon is here too. He has been along since the very beginning, joining the battalion just a month after me, at age seventeen. He's from Toronto's west end, the part where no one who is anyone lives, as my mother likes to say. Incredibly, two and a half years later, he is still a boy. He does exactly as asked, never takes the initiative, is content only to follow. He is quick with a laugh but easily takes offence and his wounded heart is visible to all. I've seen him standing bewildered in no man's land covered in a comrade's gore, trying to catch the sequence of events that brought him to such a pass. And now he is staring at the open tin of aniseed balls on the camp table and grinning like a seven-year-old.

"Take a handful, if you wish."

He dives in, aniseed balls dribbling from his fist as he stuffs his pocket. He passes half the treasure to Embree.

"It looks bad up top, sir. Do you think Fritzy may be planning something?"

"Fritzy doesn't tell me his plans, Gordon."

We are in the cellars of Cité St-Émile just outside Lens. These battered rooms are now all that remains of the workmen's houses. Last night we relieved the 116th Canadians and I am in charge of A Company. Nothing much is happening; we are simply holding the line. But the Germans have been bombarding this right frontage with Minenwerfers for the past fifteen minutes, just wanting to let us know they are still around. Embree brings no reports of death or injury; Minenwerfers go so high in the air we can see where they will land and move out of the way. They don't bother us. In fact, little does. The battalion is experienced now, hardened and formidable. Our allies are respectful, our enemies even more so. Not just of the 58th, of all Canadians. We are taller, stronger, fitter than the narrow-shouldered men I see in the columns of British soldiers – brave tommies, but pale hollow-chested creatures who grow shorter with each contingent.

There is snow on the ground. I will give my soldiers a few minutes in the warmth of the stove before we go up top to see what all the fuss is about. The sugar balls dissolve on our tongues, and we enjoy the hit of aniseed before climbing the cellar stairs and facing the December chill.

———

CIRCUMSTANCES OF DEATH REPORT

UNIT 58th Battalion
NAME Durie. W.A.P.
RANK Captain
DATE OF DEATH 29-12-17
CAUSE OF DEATH Killed in action

Detailed report of circumstances surrounding the death of this soldier
(If "Died of Wounds" please report how wounds were received):

The late Capt Durie was in command of "A" Company, 58th
Canadian Battalion in the front line, at St Emile sector, on December
29th 1917. About 9.45 a.m. the enemy began a bombardment of
"A" Co[mpan]y's frontage and support Area, using heavy Trench
Mortars. The acting C.S.M. brought in the report that a large section
of the front line had been blown in, and Captain Durie went out into
the communication trench leading towards the front line. This was
about 10.15 a.m. As he reached the top of the stairs from the dugout
and stepped aside, a large Trench Mortar struck the parados and
instantly killed Capt. Durie and several others.

His body was removed the same evening and taken out for burial in St. Pierre [Corkscrew] Cemetery, services being conducted by
Captain Ridgeway, 52nd Canadian Battalion.

(Signed) R.L. Smythe. Lt-& A/Adjt.
For Officer Commanding

PART TWO

ANNA'S WAR

⤜⤛

CANADIAN PACIFIC R'Y. CO.'S
TELEGRAPH
NIGHT LETTERGRAM
AL9WA AD
DH WSM OTTAWA 11 JAN

MRS ANNA DURIE
306 ST GEORGE ST.
TORONTO
REPLYING YOUR TELEGRAM TENTH REGRET TO CON-
FIRM CAPTAIN WILLIAM DURIE OFFICIALLY REPORTED
KILLED DEC TWENTY NINTH NINETEEN SEVENTEEN
HAVE ASKED ENGLAND FOR CIRCUMSTANCES DEATH
REPORT COPY WILL BE FURNISHED YOU IMMEDIATELY
UPON RECEIPT

DIR OF RECORDS
2.30 AM

HELEN

I was alone when the telegraph boy came to the door; Mother was somewhere in the Atlantic enjoying the New Year festivities. I had to live with my knowledge for more than a week, hold it in my heart, devise how to tell this news. I should have brought her home from the railway station into the warmth, sat her at the fire with tea, held her hand, and explained the pain. But it did not happen that way. She stepped off the train this afternoon at North Toronto, her mouth so full of Arthur's exploits and his last leave in London, poised to show me keepsakes and letters. I could only gape, my lips attempting an explanation of their blubbering. For a moment she stared, then a sound came. The sound of Lucifer thrown down into hell. I wanted her to swoon so the noises would end, but she refused to comply. Never in my life have I seen her lose control. But in that moment, all of her refinement, her breeding, her deportment vanished into the death of her son. She dropped onto all fours and began to crawl along the platform, guttural wails crashing along the walls. Her face a twisted red mask, teeth bared, mouth drooling. Everyone watching, pity and disgust moving across their faces. Her shoe lost, a tear in her dress, her hat askew, and that terrible howl, unabating.

The doctor gave her a sedative but she cries and mumbles in her sleep. I do not know how to console her.

My Heart It Is a Shrine for Deeds of His

My heart it is a shrine for deeds of his
That live for ever in an ambient light;
Like purest marble that illumined is,
Or rarest jewels in a casket white.

. . . .

I count my store; set this or that aside,
Like glittering gems, too precious to be worn:
This had its birth in Flanders; ere he died,
This proved a herald of the approaching morn.

. . . .

Meseems I taste a fragrance in the air,
A breath that hovers sweet where sunshine is:
A living thing, that comforts like a prayer,
This heart, that is a shrine for deeds of his.

Anna Durie

ANNA

When the 58th Battalion came home to Toronto a hundred thousand people lined Yonge Street to welcome them. A group of officers visited the next afternoon. His friends, names I recognized from his letters, others I had known in London. Mr. Cusler was not one of our visitors that day. The others said he was still in hospital in England, recuperating from a serious facial wound. A bullet had passed through his cheek and jaw and the required surgery was proving to be complex.

Helen and I served tea and watercress sandwiches and cakes iced with flowers, as if their conversation was to be of social engagements and the state of the weather.

They told how the three bodies were barely marked by the blast. I know that death must have come from over-pressure. It ruptures blood vessels, forcing air into the heart and brain, it smashes into every cell, it explodes colon, bowels, lungs. Arthur's poor battered lungs. The dead were each wrapped in blankets and, when darkness came, were carried to a small cemetery amid the ruins of the rail yards and mine workings – Corkscrew, named for the posts that spiralled into the ground to hold the barbed wire entanglements in place. His comrades folded his hands upon his breast, crossed his feet at the ankles. The ceremony was necessarily brief. Wooden crosses, made earlier in the day, marked the graves. I said we would visit in the summer and place his body in a coffin so he would not lie in the cold earth. They felt it fitting.

James Cobourg Hodgins
"Abbey Leix"
Brampton, Ontario
Canada
Feby 2nd 1921

Right Hon. Arthur Meighen, P. C. M. P.
Prime Minister

Dear Mr. Meighen:

I have written Mrs Durie giving my reasons for believing that what she asks is impossible. I assume that the objection comes from France, and that the cost, in the case of England, is prohibitive. With us alone I figure the cost to the country would amount finally to over $150,000,000. This we could not afford.

Mrs Durie is brilliant, lovable and erratic and her son's personality completely absorbs her. Her daughter is stability and common sense personified and I will try and work through her. I have been very plain in what I have said.

Mr Guthrie has given a negative. Of course, he is bound by precedent. I would not have written you if she had not had an interview with you.

Count on me for anything – even sacrifice.
Always cordially

James C. Hodgins

Still half an hour to pass before the two men arrived in the pony and trap promised by Captain Chanter. They would bring the coffin I chose the week before in Lens: golden oak embossed with a silver cross and its fall of tears. Helen sat on a travelling rug at the graveside. She made no sound, but I know she wept for what we were about to do.

There is a German word, *trostlos*, we should bequeath to that plain on the edge of the Souchez Valley. The *r* grates, the hollow *o*s tell of futility, and the soft *s* peters into nothingness. It means "without consolation."

The ground was torn by the jagged lines of old trenches; the walls of some had collapsed, others were cesspits for rusting equipment, rotting wood, pitiless artillery shards. Five coal mines grubbed into the earth amid the craters and the broken houses. And terrible things climbed up through the soil like stones in a garden.

A breath of wind raised the smell of cornflowers and iron from the dirt and ruffled my hair. I felt so fragile, as if the breeze might spin me over the pitheads and onto the nearest mountain of mine tailings that shadowed the land. Half a dozen railway tracks continually ran wagons through the desolation. Locomotives screamed and wheezed. It was the last quarter of the moon and the pale light caught the coal cars and glinted across their burdens, illuminating the ore into jet-black eyes raking the rows of wooden crosses. There was no boundary wall between Corkscrew British Military Cemetery and the rail yards, just a line of manicured turf. A filament of

England edged the ranks: roses, coreopsis, lavender. More than two hundred men were there facing the line they died protecting. The shell holes and the mud, though quilted with grass, exuded an unbearable ugliness.

I had used so much of my strength in the past weeks. So many things to arrange. So much greed and pettiness to allay. Fools to contend with, letters to write, money to disburse. We made few friends and many enemies. People are so afraid of questioning the rules. Even the Reverend Mollyneux asked us to leave his hostelry. "Disturbing the other guests," was the explanation he gave. The "other guests" were parents, wives, sisters: people I was trying to raise out of their complacency. "Oh yes, we agree with you," they said. "But what can you do?" A great deal. I knew I had a duty to perform not only to my son but also to those people. Their own class could not teach them. Thousands of their sons needed a voice. I told the families the graves would be obliterated, forgotten. Mine machinery and farmers' plows would churn the bodies to the surface ready to be thrown on scrap heaps. They did not want to hear. Instead they accepted the pronouncements of the Imperial War Graves Commission as if quoted from Holy Scripture. Repatriation of the dead was forbidden and instead a "higher ideal" was embodied in the war cemeteries.

We had been meticulous in our planning. Captain Chanter was most thorough. Time and again he went over every step of the operation. He was himself connected with the IWGC. He knew of their petty rules and their blind determination.

I first met him at Corkscrew Cemetery in 1919. He had been contracted by certain families to place flowers on the graves of their loved ones and so visited many of the cemeteries and spoke to a large number of visitors; an estimable man, offering his condolences, but always recognizing his place. He never intruded upon my grief but at appropriate times asked gentle questions about Arthur's life and was very interested in our family heritage. I told him of my wish to rebury my son in a coffin. The thought of him lying unprotected in the cold earth was too awful to bear. I told him of my horror of that land and of the beauty of the family plot in Toronto where his father rests. But those at the Imperial War Graves Commission had said no. I had been prepared to cover any expenses incurred. "What if everybody wanted such a thing?" they said. "There are more than a million dead." Well, what if they did? If each family would cover the cost, hire labourers, provide transportation, then why the objection?

Even in death, the army wished to control my son, to tell me how he should lie. Captain Chanter let it slip that many other families had similar problems and suggested some had even exhumed the bodies of loved ones and returned them home. I listened, not commenting, not hinting I was intrigued. Later I spoke to Helen. At first she considered it macabre and immoral. She suggested we approach senior members of our own government directly and ask for permission to bring Arthur home. His father's importance within the Canadian military and the significance of the Durie name would surely put us outside of the general rules. I acquiesced. But I told Captain Chanter I would keep in touch.

ANNA

In the months following our visit to France, I petitioned Canadian officials at every level. They expressed sympathy, then mouthed the platitudes of the Imperial War Graves Commission, as if such things concerned me. Platitudes from a group which even forbade the erection of private memorials, stating there was to be no distinction between officers and men. Instead all graves, from general's to private's, would be marked by a small stone holding the briefest of details. How could those who devised such rules understand anything? I realize a private or corporal may also have made the ultimate sacrifice, but a man's position in the world needs to be acknowledged by those who remember, for those who come after.

I wrote to the minister of militia, Mr. Hugh Guthrie, and printed five hundred leaflets for distribution throughout his riding. I contacted each of the newspapers and petitioned numerous veterans' groups. I wrote to Prime Minister Meighen, and when I received no answer wrote to his acquaintances asking them to speak to him on my behalf. Still there was no reply, and so in the autumn of 1920 Helen and I sat in the lobby of the King Edward Hotel in Toronto waiting for Mr. Meighen. It is against my nature to be so forward, to literally ambush a person, but desperate measures were required. Aides moved forward to deny me access as he emerged from the elevator, telling us to make an appointment. I informed them I was a citizen of this country and as such had every right to speak to an elected official. Meighen was an inconsequential, anaemic man but he had the grace to move them aside. We sat in the reception area and Helen and

I told the prime minister of William's work for Canada, of Arthur's heroism, of the nobility of the Duries, and of a grieving mother's wish. He listened until someone reminded him of his next appointment. He seemed most concerned and promised to look into the matter. But it was no use. Even a prime minister's opinions could not sway the bureaucracy. They refused to understand. The organizations who were united in this struggle to bring our soldiers home fell by the wayside, saying the cause was lost. The mothers and wives who protested en masse decided instead to place memorials in churches and annual remembrance notices in the newspaper. It was not enough. I would not be thwarted.

*The Honourable Hugh
Guthrie, M. P.
Minister of Militia and
Defence,
Ottawa
February 18, 1921*

*Right Hon. Arthur Meighen, P. C. M. P.
Prime Minister*

*Dear Mr Meighen:
A few days ago I received from you a letter written after you had
an interview with Mrs. Anna Durie and her daughter Miss Helen,*

seeking the privilege of bringing back the remains of their deceased son and brother to Canada.

On looking up this case I find that Mrs. Durie has been communicated with a number of times by different Officers of this Department, as well as by my predecessor. I have also communicated with Mrs. Durie, advising her that it was not in accordance with the Regulations to have her son's body brought back. I have endeavoured to secure for you a copy of the agreement made by the French and Belgian Governments, but have been unable to secure same. However, I have asked Sir George Perley to send me as soon as he can, a copy of the agreement, when I will forward same to you.

The following cable was received by the Secretary of State from the High Commissioner:

"Exhumation of bodies forbidden by special decrees of French and Belgian Governments. The opinion is that these restrictions should not be removed. The authorities recognize the sentiments with regard to the removal of bodies to their native countries, and of the strong desire in a small number of cases that exhumation should be permitted, but the reasons to the contrary appeared to the Graves Commission to be overwhelming. To allow removal by a few individuals, of necessity only those who could afford the cost, would be contrary to the principle of equality of treatment. To empty some four hundred thousand identified graves would be a colossal work and would be opposed to the spirit in which the Empire had gratefully accepted the offer made by Governments of France, Belgium, Italy and Greece to provide land in perpetuity for our cemeteries and to adopt our dead. The commission felt that a higher ideal than that of private burial at home is embodied in these war cemeteries in foreign lands where those who fought and *fell together, officers and men, lie together in their last resting place facing the line they gave their lives to maintain. They felt sure, and the evidence available to them confirmed the feeling, that the dead themselves in whom the sense of comradeship was so strong would have preferred to lie with their comrades. These British cemeteries in foreign lands would be the symbol for future generations of the common purpose, the common devotion, the common sacrifice of all ranks in an United Empire."*

I feel that if we were to depart from the Regulations in Mrs. Durie's case, it would create a very dangerous precedent.

Yours faithfully,

Hugh Guthrie M.P.

ANNA

I contacted Captain Chanter. I did not come lightly to such a decision. There was so little money and the bribes and charges would be great. The securities bequeathed by my father did not turn out as sound as I at first supposed. And William left a very small estate. During his army career his pay did not nearly cover his expenses. Much of his private fortune went into shaping the Queen's Own Rifles as the best militia unit in Canada. Maintaining the dignity of his position required substantial funds. Then suddenly he was forced into retirement, despite his most bitter objections. He was cast aside with two years' pay and no pension. I know these cares contributed to his early death. Those jealous of his name and his accomplishments were his assassins.

After his death I managed to hold onto Craigluscar for more than a decade. That handsome house in its stately grounds was my home, my right as a Durie. William's land outside the city was sacrificed to taxes. Tradespeople purloined our possessions when I could not meet their constant demands for payment. The Temperance Colonization Society, holders of the mortgage, became discourteous and finally contemptible in their attitude. But I did as I promised. Our children were raised to understand their place.

When I eventually was forced to leave Craigluscar, I rented a small house in a good neighbourhood. For the sake of Arthur and Helen, I set myself as flint against the encroachment of "Main Street," an avenue by which men and women insensibly descend into hell. And when Arthur finally bought our home on St. George Street, it was with the understanding that his inevitable rise through the bank would soon allow us larger and more fitting accommodation.

The clamour of bill collectors grew, but principles are more important than the pettiness of traders. The more I corresponded with Captain Chanter concerning a coffin, the more I recognized a bolder purpose. He told me of a Saskatchewan couple who, only two months earlier, had their hearts broken. They had one son, Grenville Hopkins, who was killed at Passchendaele just a few weeks after arriving in France. The army reported his body as missing. But the boy's comrades in the Princess Patricia's Light Infantry described to the family exactly where they had buried his remains. His parents travelled to Belgium and located the grave. A fountain pen in the young man's breast pocket, a gift from his father, confirmed identification. Such small tokens, given in love, become a link to the truth. The boy was laid in a coffin chosen by his parents and reburied at Tyne Cot Cemetery with the thousands who fell in that terrible battle.

I remember Arthur's letters from Passchendaele in which he spoke of "the blood-soaked swamps of Flanders." No. That is wrong. The letters aren't a memory. They are with me in this room. They bring me the sound of his voice, just as William's letters bring me the smell of his skin. I miss Arthur's kiss, hard and brief against my cheek, his stubble rasping my face. And my husband's, soft and breathless, or hungry. I miss my men. I miss the aroma of tobacco and empty whiskey glasses, their talk of politics and finance, their understanding of the world. I miss how their physical presence shrinks a room, the pleasure of stepping within their masculine domain. I wanted Arthur at home. He was mine and they took him from me. They destroyed my beautiful son in that awful land. They changed his name, his beliefs, even his speech. I wanted him back. I refused to be afraid.

Mr. and Mrs. Hopkins stayed for some weeks in the area and at last admitted neither could leave their son alone in a foreign land; they must take him home. But, no matter how many letters they wrote explaining their cause, the IWGC refused all requests. If things had been left to the commission, the body would still be lying unclaimed and unknown in no man's land.

Mr. Hopkins sought out the services of Captain Chanter and under cover of darkness the new coffin was opened and the remains exhumed. The party travelled all the way to

Antwerp, but unfortunately their bribes to officials were not large enough to ensure silence. Captain Chanter tells me he strongly advised Mr. Hopkins that much more should be given. The father, though I'm sure a good man, is a merchant, and so cannot possess the intelligence needed for such a complex operation. He thought he knew best. Authorities discovered the boy in a mortuary awaiting shipment with Canadian Pacific. The IWGC took possession and reburied the body in a British cemetery in the area. Private Hopkins was neither at home with his family nor at Tyne Cot with his comrades.

My decision was made. I gave the captain permission to commence the arrangements.

❧

Colonel H. T. Goodland
Dept Controller, IWGC
July 1921

Principal Asst Sec
London
With reference to the attached letter from Mrs Durie I have to report the following. Last week it was brought to my notice that a lady has been circulating a report in the Bethune district that she intended to exhume the body of her son in Bully Grenay cemetery, Corkscrew, and take it with her to Canada and subsequently the Reverend Mollyneux came to see me with the same story and also told me that owing to this lady's conduct and statements he had

asked her to leave his hostel. I advised Major Brown and asked him to give me a report on this matter and find out who this lady was and he reported that he found this lady at the Bully Grenay cemetery and she immediately jumped on him and talked a lot of irrelevant talk concerning the doings of the Commission and the War Office and all the powers that be. She also told him that if she stayed for years she would have her way and take the body away causing all sorts of letters, precedents etc from Canadian officers. After about two hours of this and after warning the lady that on no account must she touch the grave, Major Brown left. Instructions were given to the gardeners to see that this grave was not touched and to report every morning as to its condition, and he also notified the gendarmerie at the same time that this lady had expressed her intention to remove the body. This letter therefore, which I am enclosing does not probably state all that the lady wishes to say and I would ask that you please let me know what definite answer I shall make to her request. Major Brown's idea of the lady is that she is quite unreasonable and has practically lost her senses on this one subject. I mention also I think it would be a danger to allow her to do as she wishes as set out in her letter. I should be glad of your reply as soon as possible because I shall have this lady up here if there is any undue delay.

Colonel H. T. Goodland

⌘

July 14 1921
Hotel Poitier
Bully-Grenay

Colonel Goodland
Graves Commission
St. Omer

Dear Sir:
I take it for granted you will remember my name so I shall come to the object of this letter at once. Will you give me permission to exhume the body of my son Captain Durie and have him placed in a zinc coffin and reinterred in the cemetery in which his body now lies. A Toronto colonel told me he had got this permission. He exhumed his son's body and reburied it so I am not asking any-thing that has already not been granted to a Canadian family. I shall of course pay for his coffin. I hope you will understand you are dealing with a very determined woman who has suffered untold things at the hands of the IWGC. I beg to refer you to Colonel Hamilton in London and Webley here.
Yours

Mrs Anna Durie

ANNA

I was writing at the desk when that ridiculous man, Major Brown, with the puffed-up title of area superintendent, arrived at the hotel. He had the effrontery to try to tell me what I could and couldn't do. Who were these people who felt they could dictate my life? By then it was obvious there was utter confusion within the ranks of the IWGC. Placing Arthur's remains in a coffin seemed reasonable to some, others considered it out of the question. One official wrote to tell me the Corkscrew graves would be moved to another cemetery, others denied it totally. Why such subterfuge? How could I trust these people? How could the nation trust them? The previous year the French government had given way to public pressure and begun to return French soldiers to graves in their towns and villages at state expense. Why would France care about the graves of those not their own? The cemeteries would be neglected and eventually disappear. But always the IWGC was adamant: "A higher ideal than that of private burial at home is embodied in these war cemeteries in foreign lands," they said.

Such high-flown words hid their treachery and I told the major I believed it was the intention of the commission to remove all surface evidence of Corkscrew Cemetery, shifting the crosses to another cemetery but leaving the bodies. He feigned astonishment.

He had already spoken to the cemetery gardener and also to the mayor of Bully-Grenay and various police officials, confirming my declared intention to exhume Arthur. I'm sure none of them mentioned my generous bribes. I told him a great many people knew of those intentions and it was only men such as he, a bureaucrat who no doubt spent the war years safe in a London office building, who skulked around in the shadows. He at least had the grace to blush. Then he quoted statutes and regulations at me as if I were a clerk. There is a time to be blazingly truthful. I looked hard into his eyes and said the commission was composed of a set of liars and I would shoot any man who interfered with my plans. He took his leave.

A few days after his departure a notice appeared in the cemetery quoting "Article 4," forbidding anyone to disturb the graves or erect memorials. I took it from the board and walked across to the foreman gardener, who was deadheading the pelargoniums. He said not one word as I tore the paper into a hundred tiny pieces and sent them fluttering over the grass.

Bully-Grenay

Men of the soil of Bully-Grenay,
In your midst have we come, and here will we stay,
Till the stones and the chalk and the rocky bed
Yield, at our touch our glorious dead!

Swingeth a crescent moon in the sky,
With attendant star, like a torch held high;
Night winds of Summer are hushed and low,
And the pregnant moments in silence flow.

Soldiers are slumbering to left and to right,
And crosses show dim in the soft, Summer night;
Deep be your peace, who so splendidly passed,
Tho' you sleep you shall rise with the brave at the last!

Breaketh a sound on the midnight air,
And a soldier's form to our gaze is laid bare;
Boot folded on boot and with hands on his breast,
He lies like a warrior taking his rest.

Dews of the morning, touch lightly his face,
Blend with our tears in a richness of grace!
Mingled with kisses rained soft on his dust,
Revive our numbed spirit, bring healing and trust.

Lightens the East of a hallowed morn,
On a work well done, on a life new-born,
On a Sabbath of peace, on a holy day:
Farewell, forever! O sons of Grenay!

Anna Durie

ANNA

A rustle behind me and Helen's hand on my arm. The trap
pulled into the roadside, the horse snorting in the shafts. Mr.
Wheeler was there as promised, representing J.M. Currie &
Sons, the shipping agency involved in the arrangements. He
was a small man, a pinch-faced creature much smaller than
Arthur. His companion, heavy-set and greasy, bore a long scar,
rising from the collar of his shirt and twisting his jaw into
confusion. He stared at me for long moments. As they slid the
coffin from the bed of the trap and placed it near the grave
he began to grouse and grumble, unaware I could understand
every coarse French word.

"Bringing a fucking coffin is stupid. It will be seen on the
road. And zinc-lined!"

"Mrs. Durie's wishes are what is important here," Mr.
Wheeler said quietly. Then he turned to me and asked, in
French, if I had been waiting long. The other man grunted
at my fluent reply but did not apologize.

They began to section the turf and slice it from the surface, placing the long strips neatly to one side. As Helen and I
stood on the slight slope of the gravesite, they started to dig.
Sure, rapid thrusts into the dirt. Suddenly Mr. Wheeler mut-
tered softly. Only four feet down and they had hit upon a
body. Helen squeezed my hand, needing reassurance as much
as she desperately tried to reassure. I knew from his comrades
the corpse was whole, a blanket for his shroud, arms folded
on the breast. But how long does it take for flesh to decom-
pose and for bones to be clean? My daughter was frightened
by the magnitude of our task and terrified by what sights

might be revealed in that grave. Yet there are things which must be done.

The men slowed their work, digging more carefully until they abandoned the shovels and instead used trowels and brushes to uncover the remains. Mr. Wheeler inspected the blanket and declared it would hold, then the body was lifted from the depths of the earth and placed upon the grass.

I looked upon my son for the first time in nearly four years.

I had heard stories of mistakes made in the chaos of battle, of crosses placed on the wrong graves. But there was no need to check for the gap in his teeth or for the old bullet hole in his uniform. Nor to find the ivory identity disc he always wore, the black of its lettering eroded clean. The blanket that covered his head and shoulders completely, strands of wire spiking it closed, could remain in place. There would be time enough when home in Toronto to peel back the cowling and gaze upon my son. Instead I was staring at trench boots we had bought together in London the day before our final goodbye and at the distinctive lacings he always favoured: a zigzag pattern taught to him by his father. His shopping spree that day had included a new uniform ordered at Strickland and Sons in Savile Row. And a laughing visit to Buszards in Oxford Street, to partake of its famous cakes. Afterwards we sat in St. James's Park and talked about my trip home. His khaki tunic had hung too loosely on his spare form.

I know I am inclined to touch the vivid picture in my thoughts with strong colour. But I've missed his strength of mind and sound judgment for so very long, no colour could be too strong. He was a man of unusual parts. He was a Durie, as brave and noble as any of that heritage. His sister, Helen, loved learning for learning's sake. But a world much wider than the one encountered in books lay before Arthur. An alluring existence beckoned, a warrior's existence, one in which there would always be action. For him, the future held a great invisible force more enticing than all the books in the world; it challenged him to follow. And not only was this urge of youth in his blood, it was in his innermost thoughts. He did what we expected him to do. And he is gone, with all his enthusiasm.

———————

That night, in that garden, I stared at his little English boots, still laced tight upon his feet, and knew my decision was correct. Mr. Wheeler climbed from the grave and motioned the Frenchman forward.

"No," I said. "My daughter and I will place him in the coffin."

"Please, Madame. That may not be best."

But he saw my resolve and stepped aside. We lifted the blanket and its burden. He was light as air. Helen began to cry, deep wrenching sobs. I raised my eyes from his feet and saw her tears fall upon the cloth. She never faltered. We placed him in the coffin and Mr. Wheeler attached the lid. Then everything went wrong.

The men hurried toward the road, though there was no need for such haste. I knew for certain no police officer would come to investigate, no official would disturb us. I tried to keep up, to reach the mare's head so she would not be afraid. But I was too late. The Frenchman failed to compensate for

Mr. Wheeler's smaller stature; consequently the latter was holding the coffin at shoulder height. When he arrived at his destination, he tried to lower his arms but his companion simply shoved forward and the coffin fell sharply onto the bed of the trap. The startled horse, until then quietly eating roadside grass, stepped backwards, ensuring that the heavy-set man, still shoving, propelled the coffin forward. Now thoroughly alarmed, the creature reared, then twisted in the shafts. The coffin slid to the roadway with a clatter and the horse again wrenched herself fiercely against the bindings. One shaft broke away, and on the next twist its jagged remainder pierced her side. She screamed and toppled over. The Frenchman cursed and kicked at her, then began dragging at her head as if she had some choice in her fate.

"Leave her alone. Can't you see she is dying?" I said in French.

"Shit."

"I said leave her."

"I still want my money," he shouted, his spittle dancing in the moonlight. Then he left us.

Mr. Wheeler, who had simply watched the carnage, mouth agape, sat on the verge of the road, his face in his hands.

"I'm so sorry," he said. "It's not my fault. It's not my fault."

"Fault at the moment is immaterial. Please help pick up my son and return him to the cemetery."

Between the three of us we walked the coffin across the grass and placed it into the earth. When it settled onto the slightly sloped ground I heard a sudden swoosh and felt the weight shift toward the feet. Helen cried out.

"We have disturbed him. How can he ever forgive us?"

"This is what he wants us to do, Helen. You know we do not have a choice. We are doing only what is right, what is fitting."

When our work was complete the height of the coffin meant the earth mounded above the grave. Its disruption was obvious. I did not want the authorities prying open the lid; I did not want Arthur intruded on again. At least not until it was time for me to truly take him home. I wrote upon a small white card and pinned it to the sad wooden cross:

Capt W. A. P. Durie
58th Battalion CEF
(body not removed)

July 26 24
Colonel Goodland
Dept Controller
St Omer

Vice chairman
IWGC
London

Captain W.A.P. Durie, 58th Battalion, C.E.F.
Row E, Grave 21, Corkscrew British Cemetery

Mrs Durie, mother of the above named officer is back again in this country from Canada. Mr Waddington, Bethune area, reports she has been to his office and stated she is very much concerned because she has been informed by some of the employees of the mines that there is a proposal to move this cemetery and wishes to know if there is any truth in this assertion. Her address is the Hotel de Flandre, Lens, until Monday next after which she will be staying for three days at the Hotel Prince Albert, Rue St Hyacinth, Opera, Paris to which latter address a letter from you might reach her if posted in time.

Mrs Durie also told Mr. Waddington that the body of this officer would eventually rest in Canada but that she was not moving it this year. You will no doubt remember the correspondence on this subject dating back to 1921. My last letter dated Nov 3, 1921 which enclosed cuttings from Canadian papers sent me by Mrs Durie and my letter of Aug 22, 1921 enclosed a report from Major Brown, area superintendent at Bethune, with reference to the attempt she made to remove his body from Corkscrew Cemetery which was frustrated owing to an accident of the horse and cart. This lady's reappearance in the country may indicate a similar attempt to remove her son's body. I have asked Mr Waddington to endeavour to arrange that this cemetery be strictly watched as far as possible for the next few days or until we know that this lady has left the country. At the same time she might be making arrangements for some unscrupulous person to carry out this work in her absence.

Colonel Goodland

HELEN

She will not rest. Every day contains the detailed discussion of some part of her plan, even though Captain Chanter refuses to make a second attempt as long as she insists upon a coffin. He says its presence was to blame for the debacle. But Mother insists the problems stemmed from incompetent workmen and those who hired them. She instructed her lawyer to write to *all* those involved demanding the return of her bribes. We received no replies.

Each summer for the past five years we've travelled to France and England. The letter campaigns and the distribution of leaflets continue, but few people now support her cause. Time heals, and as the IWGC graveyards grow more beautiful, her accusations of indifference grow more hollow. At Corkscrew the grass is well tended and the plantings have taken to the soil. The tea roses on Arthur's grave look quite lovely. But our campanulas were removed. The rules dictate no private gardening – just as rules denied a plaque erected in his memory in Westminster Abbey, and also in Dunfermline Abbey where our ancestors once preached.

The area around the cemetery remains a wasteland. The debris of industry litters the ground. The trains shriek within a stone's throw of the crosses. Yet even in this chaos the bereaved walk quietly among the rows, weeping, deciding, as requested, on an inscription to be chiselled into the headstone. Mother wants: "He took the only way / And followed it / Unto the glorious end," but Arthur will be long gone by the time that stone is erected.

Recently our mission has become more urgent. We know Corkscrew Cemetery is to be returned to the governance of the railways and 215 bodies are soon to be moved to Loos British Military Cemetery a little way away. If we are to steal him, undetected, and make it across the ocean, it should be in the confusion of the move.

The IWGC declares it unfair to allow repatriation, that only the wealthy could afford such a course. If only they knew of our finances. We have remortgaged the house in order to afford this venture. Bills go unpaid. Men were sent to repossess the new refrigerator. I thought that I would die of embarrassment. We have changed our butcher twice because of unpaid charges and the dressmaker refused further commissions until our account was settled. Our remaining dresses are mended and then mended once more.

So many layers of fees and bribes to be dealt with: Captain Chanter himself, the police, the cemetery personnel, the labourers, the driver. Mother and I cannot try to leave France with the remains; too much is known about us. So at a cost of five hundred pounds there will be a boat waiting at Le Havre to ferry Arthur's remains across the Channel to one of the small ports on the south coast of England. He will be listed as "stores." From there he is to be taken to the left luggage office at Paddington Station. A courier, another bribe, will pass the claims ticket to us. We shall send my brother, with the remainder of our things, to Liverpool and the steamship home.

I do not want this. It is wrong. We are again to be body snatchers; we are to dig my brother's bones from the earth. But I have no voice in these matters. They consume us. There is nothing in our lives but Arthur's return. There is no reason, and this thing must be done in order for us to continue. Two women in this ugly house with only a ghost for company.

⌘

March 2 25
Anna Durie

Fabian Ware
Vice chairman, IWGC

Sir,
It was only by falsehood and misrepresentation that you could have accomplished the removal of the remains of my beloved son Captain William Arthur Peel Durie from Corkscrew Cemetery. Information from France reached me a few days ago that all the bodies had been removed, that there were none left on February 7th, yet no word has come from you or your commission either to me or to others. On the floor of the House the Honourable the Minister of Militia stated that notices would be sent by you to relatives direct. In communicating with the minister I made the misstatement that the IWGC is the most tyrannical and autocratic body of men that has existed since England lost the North American colonies. To this I would like to add, and the most dishonourable. If you will appoint a committee to investigate my case from the beginning, a committee of <u>gentlemen</u>, I shall make a great effort to go to England to give evidence before it. But if my grief and pain and the humiliation of the sacred dead are the means of restoring to the Canadian people control of their

heroic dead what has been suffered will not have been in vain. Colonel Osbourne has found it necessary to state to everyone to whom he has written on the subject that so great was the secrecy observed by you that he was in the dark and was told nothing about the matter, that my telegram was the first he heard of it. In a communication received by me from the Honourable the Minister of Militia, Ottawa, he sends me an extract from the letter from you. If, as the minister says you did, you made the statement to him that the officers in charge at St. Omer and Bethune, Colonel Goodland, an American, and Major Waddington respectively knew nothing last July about the railway which the French contemplated building through Corkscrew Cemetery and that such a course was only decided on at a conference in the Autumn I say you are telling a cold calculated lie. Your statement is unworthy of a British officer. It is not usual to find an Englishman so wanting in a sense of honour and I shall write to the Commander in Chief of the imperial forces drawing his attention to what has happened. After I had satisfied myself to the truth of the rumour and of other conditions in France I went to Bethune and saw Major Waddington. While my daughter and I were in his office he wrote a letter to Colonel Goodland repeating what I said and explaining my extreme anxiety. He requested him to write to me as soon as possible. Major Waddington's last words to me were that he would write to me if at any time the cemetery was to be removed. He also said that very shortly a brick wall was to be built at Corkscrew as had been done with other cemeteries. The cemetery was to be permanent. I confess I attributed the conditions I found in France to a want of confidence in the MacDonald government in England. I shall push this matter of the commission's brutal misrepresentation to me to the utmost limit. I beg you will not take refuge, in order to save yourself, behind *the fact that I am a deceased soldier's bereaved mother whom you wish to spare. That did not prevent you from misleading me when I could have done something to have saved the identity of my son's remains. The enclosed clippings will show you that my daughter and I and my beloved son are not without friends in Toronto.*

Yours

Mrs. Anna Durie
Widow of the late
   Lieutenant-Colonel
Durie, D.A.G.
Military District No. 2

Major Brown, a member of your staff, in 1921 was under the impression that California was in Canada. I feel sure you do not share that belief. California is one of the states in the American Union which we call United States.

ANNA

They moved him in February. A flag-draped coffin, the coffin I'd bought four years earlier. A service. A reverential procession trundling down a country road. These were the things they told me after the fact. But there was nothing I could believe of what they said. It was too late for such considerations.

How long before that new land was claimed, or before the IWGC stopped its much touted "care" and the graveyards became simply overgrown wastelands, their purpose forgotten, farmers and plows slowly encroaching, the unearthed bones piled at the hedgerows so as not to blunt the blades?

Arthur had to be with his father. He had to be in his home city where his grave would be honoured forever. Politicians mouth their platitudes about those cemeteries on foreign soil, but I knew in twenty years there would be only neglect and indifference.

They told me so many things. So many lies. At first my wish was to prevent the move, but it was hopeless. To speak to officials of the IWGC is to speak to mountebanks, snake oil salesmen. I knew for certain the Imperial War Graves Commission consisted not only of petty little men drunk on their own power, but of men possessing no morals, no breeding, and no honour. How could I be expected to trust anyone?

I had no concept how they were able to hold on to their positions. I wrote letters to newspapers in Canada and England asking for the continued care of the graves. I received official and unofficial assurances from numerous bodies. IWGC officials passed my questions around from officer to officer, each one less trustworthy than the one before. The whole organization was without morals. Even Fabian Ware, appointed as leader of the commission with much fanfare, presented me with nothing but sham and trickery.

Helen and I took a second mortgage on the house. Arthur's house, bought in 1912, as befitted his place within the city's financial community. A solid semi-detached house in the west end – not the far west end, of course, where no one of any consequence lives. I always thought we would live in a larger home after the war, when Arthur's banking career resumed. Helen's earnings as a teacher did not permit it – she was qualified to teach a number of subjects and so receive a higher salary but the principal himself was jealous of her breeding and never gave her the extra responsibility. It is reminiscent of those who conspired against Arthur and prevented an earlier promotion. Country yokels, forever envious of the city-bred, those of a status to which they could never aspire.

The mortgage money went toward payment of bribes and fees, so much higher the second time around. There had been an official watch ordered on the grave since August of the previous year, but it would give us no real cause for concern, just more money to disburse. Labourers, village policemen, government officials, customs officers: all were dealt with, and of course Captain Chanter. He was still my only link to a resolution. There was another way I could have chosen, perhaps a more civilized way, but my wishes were too well known by the summer of 1925 to allow it ever to work.

A Mr. Sutcliffe of Canada was successful in this matter. His son, Charles, had been a flying officer, killed behind enemy lines. He was buried by the Hun in a private vault in Epinoy churchyard near Cambrai surrounded by the graves of a slew of German soldiers and three Americans. In 1919 his parents asked for permission to remove the body but the family to whom the tomb belonged did not wish it to be disturbed. So there it rested until 1925 when Mr. Sutcliffe and his companion, a Mr. Pitts, convinced the prefect of the Pas de Calais that the body was that of another American. America has always allowed the repatriation of its dead. The prefect granted authority for a funeral director to carry out the exhumation with an understanding that the remains were to be transferred to New York. But from that city they simply travelled on to Lindsay, Ontario, where the boy was interred in the family vault. Everything done in daylight, with full paperwork and complete municipal approval. No subterfuge. No bribery. Except for the mysterious Mr. Pitts.

But there is little point in thinking on such matters. I could not turn back. My pain was a growing thing. Greater than acts of Parliament, than any of the laws written for those afraid to fight. I was more and more alone. So-called friends tried to persuade me to simply "honour his name." The Reverend Hodgins advised prayer. Even Helen had doubts about our cause. She pointed to the flowers in the older cemeteries, the trees beginning to show their majesty, and said perhaps Arthur would be content in such a place. No. I refused to bend.

Captain Chanter tightened his rules. He insisted I forgo the use of the coffin. He felt it had been the instrument of our problems on the last venture. I disagreed emphatically. The problem had been in the incompetence of the men. But he would not be persuaded and said a dignified but unobtrusive receptacle would be provided. Reluctantly I agreed. I would order a handsome coffin in Toronto. A brass wreath to centre the lid. It would look exceedingly well sitting in the parlour of St. George Street where I intended Arthur to lie in state. Dignitaries from the financial, military, and political worlds could pay their tributes.

We confirmed the date, the early hours of Sunday, July 26. Those in the few workmen's cottages nearby, rebuilt since the devastation of the war, would no doubt be sleeping off the excesses of Saturday night. The evening's proceedings were explained to us. Captain Chanter said the men would dig into the grave, open the original coffin, and place Arthur's remains into the smaller container. Loos Cemetery was as yet unturfed so the removal should not be obvious. In fact, Helen and I would be across the Atlantic before the IWGC realized anything had happened.

———————

I visited Arthur on the Saturday afternoon and told him of our plans. Except for the few cottages, the graveyard was surrounded by woods and old battlefields. Nearly three thousand soldiers lay there, most unidentified. Arthur was in the eastern corner, farthest from the road, the last in his row. A line of flowers already bloomed red and yellow. Headstones were not yet in place. Instead two wooden crosses marked the grave, one at its head and one at its foot. A regimental Celtic cross constructed by his fellow soldiers, and a simpler Latin cross put up by the commission. Soon he would have a more fitting memorial.

March 31 25
Colonel H. T. Goodland
Dept. Controller, IWGC

Copy to Colonel H.C. Osbourne, Canadian Agency, IWGC

Dear Mrs Durie:
I am most reluctant to cause you pain by reopening the correspondence concerning the removal of Corkscrew Cemetery. However,

in view of the letter which you addressed on the 2nd inst. to Sir
Fabian Ware I feel it a duty to make one or two points clear. First
and most important may I assure you that there is no reason
whatever for your evident fear that the identity of your son's
remains has been lost. His grave was the last to be moved. The
coffin was raised intact, covered with a Union Jack and taken to
Loos Cemetery. It was there reinterred in Plot 20, Row G, Grave
19. Second, in view of your feelings on removal, the mayor of the
commune of Loos-en-Gohelle was approached as to the prospect
of leaving Captain Durie's grave in Corkscrew Cemetery when
the others were removed. This was considered at a meeting of the
municipal council who decided that it would entail a responsibil-
ity and supervision on the part of the municipal police that could
not be assumed. I regret more than I can say your misunderstand-
ing of the character of Fabian Ware. So far from being autocratic
in a matter of this kind, he is a man of most sensitive sympathy,
one who enters deeply into the feeling of others particularly the
relatives of those who lost their lives in their country's service and
whose graves are under his care. I think I may say that the mis-
apprehensions which have caused you so much suffering have
arisen in part by reason of the fact that he personally opposed the
removal of this cemetery and forbade it as long as he could. This
evidently caused the commission's officials on the spot to give you
to understand that the cemetery would not be moved. It is un-
fortunate that you should have gained the impression that secrecy
was being observed in connection with this matter as appears from
the correspondence there has been from the first a doubt in your
own mind about the possibility of leaving Corkscrew Cemetery
in its original location. It is true that up to the time of your first

telegram to me I had not received information on the subject. No occasion had arisen from our London office to communicate with me about it. In your letter of January 28 you asked me directly to let you know whether I had heard of the project and I answered in the negative. In replying to Mr Church's letter on your behalf I said as follows: 'As a matter of fact, while I have visited a great many cemeteries, I have never personally seen Corkscrew Cemetery nor did I know that it was to be removed until I was advised by Mrs Durie. The matter had been under discussion with the French government for a long time and apparently reached a finality only at a recent date. All the information which I have communicated to Mrs Durie has been officially communicated to me by the War Graves Commission. The matter has received from first to last the close personal attention of Sir Fabian Ware, the vice chairman of the Commission. He wrote me a comprehensive and most sympathetic letter. I know that he enters deeply into Mrs Durie's feelings about the removal of her son's grave and I may add that I do so myself and have tried to make Mrs Durie feel that this is so. However, the Commission has had no choice in the matter and I can only add that Sir Fabian Ware says in the conclusion of his letter that when Mrs Durie next visits France she will find her son buried in surroundings not unworthy of a gallant soldier.'

There is I think nothing in the above nor in any other statement I have made, to the effect that I did not know about the personal removal until after the receipt of your first wire which justifies what you say to General Ware, namely that so great secrecy was observed I was in the dark and was told nothing about it. There is absolutely nothing to be concealed about the work of the

IWGC which is carried out with scrupulous and reverent care. This office is kept fully informed and I have no doubt that I would have learned the situation about Corkscrew Cemetery as soon as matters had reached a point at which it became desirable to notify me. This letter is not prompted by a desire to continue correspondence which must be very distressing to you. I only wish to clear up, if possible, any misunderstanding between us.

Goodland

ANNA

The yellow-faced man smashed into the oak, a crash of such force that a neighbourhood dog started to bark madly. Long splits appeared over the exposed lid as the hammer heaved onto the grain. The man grabbed the slats and forced each one backward until it splintered and swayed. Metal cutters sliced into the zinc lining and then his gloved hands simply tore the rest along its length. I suddenly could see Arthur's boots, perfectly preserved, and above them shreds of darkened fabric. In the lamplight I recognized the gleam of shin bones. They were twisted to one side and I remembered the slide of his body as Helen and I replaced him in the earth all that time ago.

"Shovel."

The man's companion threw it down to him, then dropped the hammer back into the tool bag. The shovel was tipped onto its edge and dragged to the right. The fabric tore and with it Arthur's joints. One heavy foot reached in and tramped on the tattered trousers. Metal scraped across the base of the coffin. As the man straightened, the blade lifted, trailing khaki and a clatter of bones. The boots, still laced, fell to the earth and I knew they still contained his feet. The lower legs were dumped into the open case, a thing of cheap fabric and brass plate, then the boots scooped up and tossed after them.

"No. Not like this."

They ignored me. A job to be completed.

The man bent again and more emerged. Oh God. An arm dangling from the metal. Finger bones dropping back into the grave.

What had I done?

"Stop. Stop. Please. Stop."

This was not as I arranged. My son was to be treated with dignity. Captain Chanter promised it would be so.

"I order you to stop."

I reached to the man and pulled at his shoulder. He shrugged me away and continued with his task. I turned to Helen for help. I was crying. More than seven years since I had cried.

She had gone. Left me to this abomination.

Sergeant Embree and Private Gordon, who died in the same moment as Arthur, watched this scene, uncomprehending.

I could hear the shovel again scraping along the metal, searching for body parts.

I demanded he stop.

Why wouldn't he stop? God, make him stop.

I lunged at the man but arms clamped around my body and lifted me away. Lifted me so easily. I could smell sweat and alcohol and tobacco, could feel the iron of his muscles. A voice in my ear, quiet and firm and threatening: "Shut up!"

"How dare you speak to me in that manner."

"We do what you paid for," he hissed. "Now shut up."

His spittle sprayed onto my face. I pushed past him, shouting to his companion, "Stop now. You will still be paid. Stop now."

Something white arced across my vision and with a hollow thud dropped into the bag. Arthur's skull.

The second man, dark as an Arab, stood over me, clutching my arm, daring me to protest, as a light came on in the far houses. The dog had awakened someone. A door opened and a wash of yellow spilled across the step. A woman appeared briefly, then she was gone. The dog still barking to the clatter of bone on bone as the valise was filled. In the depths of the grave I could see glints of white, fugitive pieces. But the men were already throwing the broken wood back into the empty tomb and filling the chasm with earth. It was done.

One carried the tool bag, the other the valise. All I could do was follow. Helen cowered, a dark mass among the roadside vegetation. She knelt, her head curled to the earth, her two arms wrapped in opposite directions around her head, so she could neither see nor hear. When one man roughly touched her spine she stayed in place. Only when I smoothed her hair did she look up, her face a curtain of tears. We climbed into the back seat of the motor, the Arabic man pushing a little, attempting to prod us into speed. He threw the valise onto the floor next to us. Arthur rattled into stillness.

[Translated from the French.]

This day, 4 September, 1925, 4:20 p.m.

We, the undersigned, Louis Rey, captain, and Fernand Dejardin, foot officer, in the town of Lievin, department of Pas-de-Calais, in our official capacity and following the orders of our superiors, being at our police station with:

Monsieur How, Henri, Georges, age forty-three years, head gardener of the English cemetery at Loos-en-Gohelle, resident at rue Hoche, at the house of Monsieur Denous, Gaston, declares:

"I am charged with surveillance and maintenance of the tombs in the British Military Cemetery, rue de Lens, Loos-en-Gohelle. On 25 July, 1925, towards 8 p.m., I did a tour of inspection of the cemetery and assured myself that nothing abnormal was to be found. Nothing suspicious could be seen. The next morning, 26 July, 1925, around 8:30 a.m. I did my round of the cemetery. Arriving at the seventh row of graves and facing that of Captain Durie, 58th Canadian Battalion, I noticed that the surrounding earth had been recently disturbed. To the side were the newly formed footprints of a woman and two men which I supposed were formed during the night. As this was abnormal, I asked the woman in a nearby house if she had heard anything. She said that her dog had barked very loudly for two hours and that she got up, but saw nothing. I informed Monsieur Cowan, head gardener for the English Military Cemeteries in the district of Loos-en-Gohelle. I have seen nothing else abnormal in the cemetery. No one has asked questions regarding the movement of the bodies of British soldiers. I did not give information to anyone. Foreign visitors are often in the cemetery."

The statement was presented to and signed by: How. . . .

————————

Monsieur Grinham, François, age thirty-four years, horticultural officer of the Bethune sector, British camp, rue du Moulin-Mascelt, declares:

"On July 26, 1925, toward 12 o'clock, I received information from Monsieur Cowan, gardener at Loos-en-Gohelle, that the earth covering the tomb of Canadian Captain Durie, buried at the British cemetery at that location, rue de Lens, had been disturbed by persons unknown. The tomb was the object of a special surveillance. I concluded that someone had renewed their attempts to exhume the body. About two years ago a similar attempt failed. I reported to Major St-Victor, Under-Intendant of the British sector of Bethune. Accompanied by him, I returned to that place where I saw the disturbance to the earth. The imprints of the feet of a woman and of men were formed on the borders of Captain Durie's tomb. That same day, without authorization to dig into the tomb, it was impossible to assess whether the body of Captain Durie was in place. We asked for authorization to dig from the central office in St-Omer, who passed the request to the necessary offices in London.

"Today, 4 September, 1925, I received the order from Deputy Controller Goodland, resident at St-Omer, to open the tomb in question in order to find if the body of Captain Durie was present. Arriving at the coffin we were shocked to see that the cover was broken, the zinc was ripped along its full length, and the casket was empty. Some clothing debris and pieces of bone remained. The bones constituting the skeleton had disappeared. I did not know who had committed this malevolent act. I then reported the information to you regarding the violation of the tomb."

The statement was presented to and signed by: Grinham. . . .

———————

On 27 July, 1925, the Lievin gendarmerie was informed by the British Authorities (Maintenance of the Military Cemeteries in France) that it was interested in inspecting the tomb of Canadian Captain Durie because of the attempted exhumation of the body, presumably carried out by that officer's mother. On that date the tomb was intact and the authorities charged with its maintenance had not received special authorization from London to open the tomb and assure themselves the body of Captain Durie could be found there.

Since 15 August, 1924, after receipt of letter 3167 from the Adjutant General of the General Command, 1st Region, Lille, the gendarmerie had conducted a special surveillance of the cemetery at Loos-en-Gohelle both day and night where the body of Captain Durie lay; they never saw anything unusual.

During our investigations it was impossible to discover the least information, as the police and the local authorities in the immediate vicinity of Loos-en-Gohelle found nothing that indicated the authors of this exhumation.

———————

Mrs Durie and Miss Helen Durie, St. George Street, were passengers on the steamship *Megantic*, from Liverpool, having paid a short visit to France and England. They arrived home yesterday morning.

"Social Events," *The Globe*, Monday, August 17, 1925

ANNA

I do not recognize the woman in the glass. My skin is paper-thin, stretched so tightly across my bones it must surely tear. My eyes are hollow, my hair limp and thin. It hurts to wear my dentures, so my mouth is an empty puckered hole. William said I was the prettiest girl in all of Canada. He would turn me to the sunlight and draw his fingers through the red of my hair, laughing at the colours moving along its length. Now I am the colour of trespass.

For eight years this cancer has grown inside me. I knew of its existence as I sat by his coffin in the front room of the house on St. George Street. He lay in state for three days as people came to call. The talk was of his bravery, his sacrifice, his honour. But all I knew was the memory of his boots falling to the earth, dragging his ankle joints apart. He was my beloved son and I dishonoured him. I could feel the blackness beneath my rib cage – a tiny wound no bigger than a bullet, oozing its poison into my breast.

Our passage home on the *Megantic* was not the jubilant journey I had envisaged. I had work to complete. The hideous things those men had done to his body needed to be assuaged. In London I had bought the finest linen and cut it into narrow strips, each piece exactly sixty-nine and a half inches long. In that same store I purchased a bolt of pure Sea Island cotton, the kind once used for Queen Victoria's handkerchiefs, so light they could float in the air like a feather. I scoured the streets and bought fenugreek and fragrant thyme and three small bunches of lavender to mix with cloves, cedar bark, and sage. Oil of orange and oil of lemon completed my needs. Helen was banished to the public rooms, and in the ship's cabin I began my reparation.

I spread one length of cotton along the bed and opened the suitcase that held my son. My hand dipped inside to touch him, the first time since that day he had leaned from the train window to roughly kiss my cheek and I had covered his hand with mine and told him of my love. He said farewell and vanished, smiling, from this life of mine. Now I lifted the pieces of him from out of the darkness. Each bone was rubbed with scented oils, then placed in situ upon the sheet. Some flesh remained on the pelvic bone and on one femur, but it had turned to a grey-white wax. Some upon his right cheek fell away as I worked. Where the markings of the shovel showed fresh I spent time soothing the blemish with citrus. Not all of him was present. Three fingers and the base of his spine were missing, still resting in that broken coffin. I sprinkled herbs and spices into the hollows and plains of his skeleton and slowly the odour of the grave dissipated. The long linen strips wound around him and at places within the windings I laid his buckle and buttons, the lacings of his boots, the 58th insignia, my engagement ring, my diamond brooch – a present from his father, my gold locket – a present from my father. When each piece was ready, I placed it upon the cotton within the soft nest of my trunk. Between the bones I set the remains of his uniform, the scraps of serge and leather. A final sheet of cotton then covered him and onto that I weighted all but one of my dresses.

It was not enough. Rituals for a hero cannot cleanse the priestess. Nothing could assuage the deed. I watched my son's limbs swing from the end of a labourer's shovel, saw his skull roll in the dirt. What honour did I give?

———————

IWGC

London

May, 1930

Captain W.A.P. Durie, 58th Battalion, C.E.F.
Loos British Military Cemetery
Plot 20, Row G, Grave 19.

Reference Major Kinnear's ch3414/r dated 17 April, 1930

It is agreed that the particulars relating to the burial of the above named officer should be deleted from the certified documents and registrar for the above named cemetery.

HELEN

The French wanted to prosecute but the IWGC desired to hide our crimes – even from their own people. In October 1928, a headstone was erected over Arthur's empty grave by some department ignorant of what had occurred, and the finance section wrote to us asking for payment of thirteen shillings, eight pence to cover the cost of the chosen inscription. We frightened them. Senior officers, all primped and polished, terrified of two women. They thought our triumph would precipitate a whole rabble of Canadians demanding to dig up their sons.

In Toronto, people expressed much pleasure at our success in finally receiving permission to bring Arthur's body home – that was the story we told. But we could see the veiled resentment. Some army personnel even refused to attend the funeral, saying such privilege was wrong. We told no one of our actual deeds.

And those deeds failed to alleviate my mother's suffering. In one of her poems about Arthur – there are many – Mother asks if there can be a balm for her grief, a way to ease her pain. "As tigress torn from cub may find / Ere she shall see her young again?" So many years since we buried him here in St. James Cemetery and yet she has never turned to me as that balm. She topped Arthur's grave with a dark, flat stone outlining his war record. It was not enough. An eight-foot-tall cross of sacrifice now partners it – and ensures our money troubles have not ended. But still it did not soothe her.

I do as she asks. I will not speak to any pupil at Jarvis Collegiate who chooses to take German classes; they may attend my English course but I will not acknowledge them. And when the school decided to erect a plaque to those students and teachers who fought in the Great War and survived, I joined her campaign against such "abomination." We lost the fight. But no matter what I do, my role is as her companion in grief and revenge, never her succour.

I had to sell the St. George Street house to satisfy our creditors. Debts replaced by other debts, but it gave us time to breathe. Mother says I must marry well and our financial problems will be solved. I am fifty years old. There will be no husband in my life. It is a very long time since I was courted by a man, since I was kissed, since a London afternoon when Arthur was alive and all manner of things seemed possible.

Morning

Come to me, hero of my dreams,
When sleep upon mine eyes descends;
When starlight through my curtain streams,
Bring liquid peace that sorrow ends.

. . . .

Come to me when Death's kindly mists
Are dimming eyes that look for you;
Come, if weak nature still resists
The iron clasp, the chilling dew.

Anna Durie

ANNA

Elmo Cusler came to see me last week. His limp is quite pronounced and his cheek heavily scarred. But he is still a handsome man, though there is a sadness to his face that comes not only from the drag of rigid tissue against his lip. He is a bank manager now and chairman of the 58th Battalion's historical committee. I would have survived the visit, exchanged a few pleasantries, even coped with the constant references to "Bill" if I hadn't glanced from the window and seen his young daughter waiting in the car. She must be about twelve years old. She was staring at the house, chewing on a ribboned pigtail and willing her father to reappear. A pretty child with wide eyes as dark as Cusler's. Arthur once let slip the power of Cusler's eyes: "Like a gypsy. Always reading my soul." He saw my glance and began to talk about his daughter. How spoiled she was by his sisters and brother who had no children of their own, how she still believed he could do no wrong, how much delight he took in her presence. It wasn't fair. Arthur's child should come to visit here. I should be serving my own granddaughter hot chocolate and talking of Christmas gifts. I should be teaching her to needlepoint and telling her the myths of the Old World. Arthur would be a bank manager. No. In the executive offices by now. His wife would consult me on how to handle their sons, bundles of mischief who could already ride like the wind. We would spend the holiday in England at her family's estate, then travel to the south of France, so good for Arthur's lungs.

Cusler was talking about his daughter still. His eyes smiling. How dare he? Why should he have this joy, this privilege?

Why did a jumped-up nobody survive while Arthur died? Because he hid in those deep cellars, afraid of the shells while Arthur braved the mayhem. Because he was terrified of the Hun, going to hospital for the slightest scratch, while Arthur stayed to face the guns. He was a craven coward, a shirker, a spineless poltroon worse than those who never went to fight, worse than those to whom I gave white feathers on the street. He deserved to be shot, his war record of lies expunged, and never should he presume to even visit my son's grave, never even mention his name.

"You are Judas. You left him to die while you cringed like a rat in the darkness."

Cusler's face was white, the scars vivid slashes of red. Oh God. I said those things aloud. All of those things. Helen stood at the door, her mouth agape. Major Cusler stared at me, his jaw rigid. Our differences forbade him to answer: I am a woman, old, of a higher class than him, ill, dying. I am grieving for his friend, for my son. At Arthur's funeral Cusler's body shook as he stood at the graveside and his eyes were wet, but he has never seen me weep – he knows my strength. He rose. One nod of his head, slow and controlled, then he turned sharply and walked from the room. I could hear Helen's urgent murmur, but he did not reply. The front door clicked shut and I saw him, ramrod straight, cross the grass and enter his motor car. The child jabbered in his ear but he seemed to make no response to her prattle. He was gone.

I cannot telephone. I cannot write to him.

I do not have the words.

I cannot bend.

I have not travelled to Europe since 1925 but I have seen newspaper photographs of the cemeteries. The stones shining white, footed by colour. There are always visitors. Not just to see the graves of those they lost, but also to walk among the headstones, weeping at the words.

Helen will continue to visit Arthur's grave here at St. James. She will lay flowers on his tomb. But when she dies there will be no one left to make a remembrance and only the gardener will tend the grave. She never married. Perhaps I should not have turned young men away from our door. But I always felt she might do better than a mere Toronto man. She grows short with me as the days pass. I think she is angry I am dying. Angry I am leaving her alone. I gave my attention to Arthur, in his life and in his death. There will be no grandchildren. The face in the glass is all there is.

A Bugle Call

Give me back the years of wonder,
Bring again the days of war!
Let me feel my pulses throbbing,
Close my ears to children's sobbing,
And my life of sorrow robbing,
Take away the days that are.
Give me back the years of wonder,
Bring again the days of war!

. . . .

Anna Durie

A long, long time ago – if I were there then, I wouldn't be there now; if I were there now and at that time, I would have a new story or an old story, or I might have no story at all – there came a season of sadness. The four corners of the sky collapsed and the world and all its regions burst apart. Fires raged across the shattered land. Flood waters tumbled through the gaping maw. Savage beasts preyed upon the innocent and considered life to be worthless. The goddess Nü Wa, she who created men from clay, cut the legs from a giant turtle to support the corners of the heavens and blended rocks of five colours to mend the cracks in the sky. She quenched the fires and dammed the flood with ashes of reeds. She taught the beasts and birds and insects to do no harm to one another. And she instructed the people of that land to henceforth dwell in peace. Nü Wa rode above the clouds in a chariot drawn by three dragons to gather up the earth's ghosts who had died in that season of sadness, crowds beyond number. She transported them to the ninth heaven where the beauties of the afterlife awaited them beneath the deepest water.

ACKNOWLEDGEMENTS

Access to the diaries and letters of the men and officers of the 58th Battalion gave me a glimpse into the private world of those who lived beside Bill Durie. I am immensely grateful to the families who allowed the use of their papers and photographs, including Jane Cusler, who was the pigtailed little girl in the car waiting for her father in 1933; Douglas Cosbie Ware, who fondly remembers his grandfather Dr. Gerry Cosbie; and Neil Affleck, who picked up an old copy of *Toronto Life* in a dental office and recognized his grandfather's battalion. Arnold Jukes's nephews, Don and Ernest, and Geoff Stead, nephew of Dick Joyce, also gave invaluable help.

Gord MacKinnon, of the Friends of the Canadian 58th Battalion, generously supplied me with a copy of the battalion's War Diary and other preliminary research documents. Kevin Shackleton, author of *Second to None: The Fighting 58th Battalion of the Canadian Expeditionary Force*, allowed full access to his files. His book gives a comprehensive examination of the men and officers who went from enthusiastic amateurs to tough, battle-savvy veterans. I have taken the liberty of delving into the Duries' private thoughts, but the battles, exact locations, and timing of events are all factual. Both Shackleton and MacKinnon read the manuscript to verify military accuracy. Every man named in *The Invisible Soldier* is an actual member of the battalion whose family papers or army records I have used in order to discover his individual humanity.

The National Archives of Canada, the Imperial War Museum, the Public Records Office in England, and the Queen's Own Rifles gave crucial assistance. I am deeply indebted to the City of Toronto Archives, especially manager Karen Teeple. The Commonwealth War Graves Commission in Maidenhead, Berkshire, quite literally opened its offices to me, providing space and time in which to examine the vast files it holds on the Durie case and related matters. In 1931 a *Sunday Express* headline read: "British War Dead Smuggled." The article detailed a lucrative traffic in the bodies of Allied soldiers. The commission conducted a thorough investigation and concluded that only Durie and Major Charles Sutcliffe were ever successfully spirited across the Channel; other tales were mere adulterated versions of their stories.

John Daly travelled across London to peer at ancient newspaper type; Janna Worthington translated the French criminal investigation documents; and Linda Gard, who now owns the Durie house on St. George Street, showed me the rooms and staircases where Bill, Anna, and Helen once roamed.

Angie Gardos, managing editor at *Toronto Life*, was the first to recognize a fascinating story and kept on wanting more. Gary Ross of the late, lamented publishing firm Macfarlane Walter & Ross knew the magazine article must be a book and encouraged me through the transition, and Jonathan Webb, associate publisher at McClelland & Stewart, and copy editor Barbara Czarnecki showed me the path through the final terrors. I would like to thank the Ontario Arts Council for grants which allowed the luxury of time.

PHOTO CREDITS

Anna Peel, 1879: City of Toronto Archives, Fonds 1065, Series 833, File 01, Image 04

Lt.-Col. William S. Durie: City of Toronto Archives, Fonds 1065, Series 833, File 02, Image 06

Craigluscar: City of Toronto Archives, Fonds 1065, Series 833, File 01

Arthur as a boy: City of Toronto Archives, Fonds 1065, Series 833, File 02, Image 01

Lt. W.A.P, Durie, 1915: University of Toronto Archives, A1965-0002

Arthur, Anna, and Helen: City of Toronto Archives, Fonds 1065, Series 833, File 03, Image 02

Anna Durie, c. 1915: City of Toronto Archives, SC65, Box 3, File 1

Helen Durie, 1914: City of Toronto Archives, Fonds 1065, Series 833, File 02, Image 03

Officers of the 58th: Canada 3rd Contingent

Arthur and companions, 1917: City of Toronto Archives, SC65, Box 3, File 4

Lt. Elmo Cusler: Courtesy Jane Cusler

Dr. Jack Affleck: Courtesy Neil Affleck

"Juksie": National Archives of Canada, PA7377

Wemyss Castle: City of Toronto Archives, Fonds 1065, Series 832, File 11

"Ginger": http://users.pandora.be/aandeschreve/ginger.ht

Anna in mourning: City of Toronto Archives, Fonds 1065, Series 833, File 02, Image 05

Anna at Corkscrew: City of Toronto Archives, Fonds 1065, Series 833, File 04, Image 02

Loos cemetery: Veronica Cusack

St. James' cemetery: Veronica Cusack